Global Perspectives on Social Media in Tertiary Learning and Teaching:

Emerging Research and Opportunities

Inna Piven
Unitec Institute of Technology, New Zealand

Robyn Gandell
Unitec Institute of Technology, New Zealand

Maryann Lee
Unitec Institute of Technology, New Zealand

Ann M. Simpson
Unitec Institute of Technology, New Zealand

A volume in the Advances in
Educational Technologies and
Instructional Design (AETID) Book
Series

Published in the United States of America by
    IGI Global
    Information Science Reference (an imprint of IGI Global)
    701 E. Chocolate Avenue
    Hershey PA, USA 17033
    Tel: 717-533-8845
    Fax: 717-533-8661
    E-mail: cust@igi-global.com
    Web site: http://www.igi-global.com

Library of Congress Cataloging-in-Publication Data

Names: Piven, Inna, 1971- author. | Gandell, Robyn, 1959- author. | Lee,
    Maryann, 1971- author. | Simpson, Ann M., author.
Title: Global perspectives on social media in tertiary learning and teaching:
    emerging research and opportunities / By Inna Piven, Robyn Gandell,
    Maryann Lee, and Ann M. Simpson.
Description: Hershey PA : Information Science Reference, [2018] | Includes
    bibliographical references.
Identifiers: LCCN 2017057029| ISBN 9781522558262 (hardcover) | ISBN
    9781522558279 (ebook)
Subjects: LCSH: Social media in education--New Zealand. | Internet in higher
    education--New Zealand. | Education, Higher--Effect of technological
    innovations on--New Zealand.
Classification: LCC LB1044.87 .P525 2018 | DDC 371.33--dc23 LC record available at https://
lccn.loc.gov/2017057029

This book is published in the IGI Global book series Advances in Educational Technologies and
Instructional Design (AETID) (ISSN: 2326-8905; eISSN: 2326-8913)

British Cataloguing in Publication Data
A Cataloguing in Publication record for this book is available from the British Library.

For electronic access to this publication, please contact: eresources@igi-global.com.

Advances in Educational Technologies and Instructional Design (AETID) Book Series

ISSN:2326-8905
EISSN:2326-8913

Editor-in-Chief: Lawrence A. Tomei, Robert Morris University, USA

MISSION

Education has undergone, and continues to undergo, immense changes in the way it is enacted and distributed to both child and adult learners. From distance education, Massive-Open-Online-Courses (MOOCs), and electronic tablets in the classroom, technology is now an integral part of the educational experience and is also affecting the way educators communicate information to students.

The **Advances in Educational Technologies & Instructional Design (AETID) Book Series** is a resource where researchers, students, administrators, and educators alike can find the most updated research and theories regarding technology's integration within education and its effect on teaching as a practice.

COVERAGE

- Social Media Effects on Education
- Game-Based Learning
- Web 2.0 and Education
- E-Learning
- Higher Education Technologies
- Classroom Response Systems
- Collaboration Tools
- Digital Divide in Education
- Virtual School Environments
- Curriculum Development

IGI Global is currently accepting manuscripts for publication within this series. To submit a proposal for a volume in this series, please contact our Acquisition Editors at Acquisitions@igi-global.com or visit: http://www.igi-global.com/publish/.

Titles in this Series

For a list of additional titles in this series, please visit:
https://www.igi-global.com/book-series/advances-educational-technologies-instructional-design/73678

Curriculum Internationalization and the Future of Education
Semire Dikli (Georgia Gwinnett College, USA) Brian Etheridge (Georgia Gwinnett College, USA) and Richard Rawls (Georgia Gwinnett College, USA)
Information Science Reference • ©2018 • 360pp • H/C (ISBN: 9781522527916) • US $195.00

Handbook of Research on Integrating Technology Into Contemporary Language Learning...
Bin Zou (Xi'an Jiaotong-Liverpool University, China) and Michael Thomas (University of Central Lancashire, UK)
Information Science Reference • ©2018 • 626pp • H/C (ISBN: 9781522551409) • US $265.00

Technology Management in Organizational and Societal Contexts
Andrew Borchers (Lipscomb University, USA)
Information Science Reference • ©2018 • 365pp • H/C (ISBN: 9781522552796) • US $195.00

Engaging Adolescent Students in Contemporary Classrooms Emerging Research and...
Prathiba Nagabhushan (St. Mary MacKillop College, Australia)
Information Science Reference • ©2018 • 216pp • H/C (ISBN: 9781522551553) • US $135.00

Impact of Learning Analytics on Curriculum Design and Student Performance
Manoj Kumar Singh (Mekelle University, Ethiopia) Zenawi Zerihun (Mekelle University, Ethiopia) and Neerja Singh (Ram Manohar Lohia Avadh University, India)
Information Science Reference • ©2018 • 215pp • H/C (ISBN: 9781522553694) • US $175.00

Integrating Multi-User Virtual Environments in Modern Classrooms
Yufeng Qian (Northeastern University, USA)
Information Science Reference • ©2018 • 342pp • H/C (ISBN: 9781522537199) • US $185.00

Written Corrective Feedback for L2 Development Emerging Research and Opportunities
Qi Guo (Baoji University of Arts and Sciences, China)
Information Science Reference • ©2018 • 167pp • H/C (ISBN: 9781522551034) • US $125.00

For an entire list of titles in this series, please visit:
https://www.igi-global.com/book-series/advances-educational-technologies-instructional-design/73678

701 East Chocolate Avenue, Hershey, PA 17033, USA
Tel: 717-533-8845 x100 • Fax: 717-533-8661
E-Mail: cust@igi-global.com • www.igi-global.com

Table of Contents

Chapter 6
Future Directions: Emergent Social Media Technologies and the Potential for
Ann M. Simpson, Unitec Institute of Technology, New Zealand

Preface

Working together over the last two years as part of a team of learning designers in a course development unit, the authors came to realize the extent of social media use in tertiary education. At the same time, they began to recognize that although research into use of social media in education was increasing, there seemed to be a few investigations into students and lecturers' perceptions of their use of social media. Many studies appeared to focus on social media for a specific purpose and investigate the effectiveness of this specific use in learning and teaching. Moreover, research on the use of social media in education for Māori and Indigenous communities is limited.

As part of the course development unit the authors worked closely with lecturers from a wide range of programs (business, sport, health, education and trades), from pre-degree, degree to post-graduate study and with a hugely diverse student population. We began to realize that a number of these lecturers were using social media in their teaching but that the stories they told about their teaching and the students experiences did not necessarily match the stated intent for the use of social media in their learning and teaching. The following questions began to surface: What was the lecturers' motivation to use social media in their teaching? Did the expectations of lecturers meet the reality of using social media? How did students engage with use of social media in a classroom setting? What pedagogical cultural frameworks are required when using social media with Māori and Indigenous students?

From these initial questions we have gathered our research into this book to answer the question What was the lived experience for lecturers, academics and students using social media in their learning and teaching? This research provides new perspectives on the use of social media in tertiary education by exploring a range of ways that social media has been implemented in learning and teaching practice. In addition, two chapters focus on how social media can be used in ways that support Maori and Indigenous students highlighting key Kaupapa Māori principles. As the use of social media by tertiary lecturers increases it is important to understand the possibilities of this use of social media as well as the realities for students and lecturers.

This book is intended for tertiary educators who are interested in the implications of using social media for learning and teaching. Although primarily focused on tertiary education, this book may be of interest to other providers and stakeholders within the education sector and Indigenous communities. The chapters cover wide range topics reflecting the broad-spectrum of interests and experiences of the authors. The chapters in this book may be read independently. However, chapters 3 and 4 are designed to be read together in order to provide a broader context for, and understanding of, the complex issues addressed within the field of social media and Māori and Indigenous communities. Each chapter concludes with a section on key words and definitions to help the reader to gain a better understanding of the pedagogical and social media concepts introduced in the book. The book is organized in the following way:

Chapter 1: *Social Media in Tertiary Education – Considerations and Potential Issues* reviews important concepts, possible pedagogies and potential educational contexts related to social media use in the higher education classroom. This is an introductory chapter that serves as a point of departure for readers. It presents some themes that will be explored in further detail in the following chapters.

Chapter 2: *Facebook in the International Classroom* explores international students' learning experiences with two undergraduate business courses delivered in a blended format with the use of social media. Emerging from the points of view and experiences of international students, this study looks at educational values of Facebook for collaboration, self-directed learning and professional development.

Chapter 3: *Navigating the Social Media Space for Māori and Indigenous Communities* explores how Māori and Indigenous communities are engaging in social media in ways that reflect their cultural aspirations and Indigenous ways of being. Social media provides opportunities for Indigenous people to represent an Indigenous worldview that encompasses their cultural, political and social preferences. Highlighted also in this chapter are the risks inherent within the use of social media for Māori and Indigenous communities. This chapter is designed to preface chapter four, as it provides a broader context about Indigenous use of social media and identifies a number of benefits and challenges.

Chapter 4: *A Kaupapa Māori Facebook Group for Māori and Indigenous Doctoral Scholars* is examining the use of Facebook to support Māori doctoral scholars and academics. Through gaining perspectives from three senior Māori academics who administer the site - Dr Mera Lee-Penehira, Dr Jen Martin and Dr Hinekura Smith, this research seeks to identify key Kaupapa Māori elements that underpin the Facebook group. It also highlights ways in which members engage with each other as Māori Indigenous academics to support their doctoral journeys.

Chapter 5: *Using Social Media in Creating and Implementing Educational Practices* investigates lecturers and learning designers' uses of social media in course design and delivery through a qualitative research study. The main themes from the analysis, and relevant pedagogies that emerged in this study, are discussed.

Chapter 6: *Future Directions – Emergent Social Media Technologies and the Potential for Higher Education* concludes the discussion about social media in tertiary education by looking at evolving nature of the technologies and practices available in today's teaching and learning context as well as ones that are considered to impact higher educational learning and teaching in the future.

Acknowledgment

The authors wish to individually acknowledge their friends, family, and professional networks in reverse alphabetical order.

Ann M. Simpson

For me, the term 'acknowledgements' is an underwhelming word that doesn't quite describe the level of support received while undertaking this project. I have admired the collegial discussion, mutual support and guidance throughout this process by my co-authors, a very talented group of researchers and women. I would like to thank the publishers, the reviewers, the proof-readers (Jane and Chris), and most importantly, you, the readers of this book, without whom the implications are obvious. I would like to thank my extended family Mom, Dad (posthumously), Susan, Noell (posthumously), Adrienne and Dave. I'd like to thank my friends – Karen, Sarah, and Mark - who continued to listen to me about my challenges with this book, who helped me through inexplicable life events and who tolerated my quirky schedule. I'd also like to thank Margaret and Tom for their interim supervision and steadfast belief in me. Finally, and most especially, I'd like to extend my heartfelt gratitude to my immediate family, Pete, Katelyn, John and Poppy for their continued devotion and encouragement.

Inna Piven

Many people, in one way or another, supported and encouraged me all the way through writing this book, which I must say was one of the most ambitious projects I have ever been involved in. First, I am extremely grateful to my co-authors, talented teachers and learning designers with whom I had the opportunity to share research interests. Their reliability and camaraderie made the book writing process enjoyable and rewarding. I wish to acknowledge the support received from my colleague Henry Ho, an Associate Professor at Ferris State University (Michigan, USA) who contributed significantly to our research on international students' learning experience. I am indebted to my family, my husband Dmitry and my daughter Sofia, who have never failed to support me and always were the first, and most attentive readers of chapter drafts. I also thank my family in Russia (Mom, Dad, Alex) for being good listeners and putting up with my overdue calls. A special thanks goes to Jamie Denton for insightful discussions about social media, stimulating comments and much-needed feedback. Finally, I thank our publisher and, specifically, Courtney Tychinski for supporting this book and patiently tolerating our deadlines for submissions.

Maryann Lee

I would like to thank my co-writers Inna Piven, Ann Simpson and Robyn Gandell alongside my two colleagues Jane Scott and Maureen Perkins for providing me with valuable editorial feedback and support. I would like to acknowledge Mera Lee-Penehira, Hinekura Smith and Jen Martin not only for the time they contributed as research participants, but also for their ongoing work as Māori academic women supporting a range of Kaupapa Māori initiatives, including the MAI ki Tāmaki Facebook Group. I would also like to thank my sister Jenny Lee who continues to guide my work as an emerging researcher. Lastly, I would like to acknowledge my daughter Hine Pehia Lee-Hohaia and her many cousins, all of whom provide both a premise and a motivation for me engaging in this work of Kaupapa Māori research.

Robyn Gandell

Writing this book has been a very collegial exercise and my first thanks go to my co-authors who have provided constant positive support throughout our research and writing processes. These amazing women have never failed to offer help and encouragement and it has been a privilege to work with them. Thanks to my co-researcher Inna for her vision and determination, Maryann for her wonderful insights and discussions, and Ann for her hard work and positivity. In addition, I would like to thank our proof readers and advisors Jane and Chris for their attention to detail and their patience with our shortcomings. Finally, a huge thanks to my family, my children Daniel and Camille, for always believing in me, making me dinner and intermittently helping clean the house, and my father Gordon, who sadly died this year, my mother Jill, and my sisters, Tina, Sandra and Chelle, for their support in all aspects of my life which made writing this book possible.

The authors wish to individually acknowledge their friends, family, and professional networks in reverse alphabetical order.

For me, the term 'acknowledgements' is an underwhelming word that doesn't quite describe the level of support received while undertaking this project. I have admired the collegial discussion, mutual support and guidance throughout this process by my co-authors, a very talented group of researchers and women. I would like to thank the publishers, the reviewers, the proof-readers (Jane and Chris), and most importantly, you, the readers of this book, without whom the implications are obvious. I would like to thank my extended family Mom, Dad (posthumously), Susan, Noell (posthumously), Adrienne and Dave. I'd like to thank my friends – Karen, Sarah, and Mark - who continued to listen to me about my challenges with this book, who helped me through inexplicable life events and who tolerated my quirky schedule. I'd also like to thank Margaret and Tom for their interim supervision and steadfast belief in me. Finally, and most especially, I'd like to extend my heartfelt gratitude to my immediate family, Pete, Katelyn, John and Poppy for their continued devotion and encouragement.

Many people, in one way or another, supported and encouraged me all the way through writing this book, which I must say was one of the most ambitious projects I have ever been involved in. First, I am extremely grateful to my co-authors, talented teachers and learning designers with whom I had the opportunity to share research interests. Their reliability and camaraderie made the book writing process enjoyable and rewarding. I wish to acknowledge the support received from my colleague Henry Ho, an Associate Professor at Ferris State University (Michigan, USA) who contributed significantly to our research on international students' learning experience. I am indebted to my family, my husband Dmitry and my daughter Sofia, who have never failed to support me and always were the first, and most attentive readers of chapter drafts. I also thank my family in Russia (Mom, Dad, Alex) for being good listeners and putting up with my overdue calls. A special thanks goes to Jamie Denton for insightful discussions about social media, stimulating comments and much-needed feedback. Finally, I thank our publisher and, specifically, Courtney Tychinski for supporting this book and patiently tolerating our deadlines for submissions.

Acknowledgment

I would like to thank my co-writers Inna Piven, Ann Simpson and Robyn Gandell alongside my two colleagues Jane Scott and Maureen Perkins for providing me with valuable editorial feedback and support. I would like to acknowledge Mera Lee-Penehira, Hinekura Smith and Jen Martin not only for the time they contributed as research participants, but also for their ongoing work as Māori academic women supporting a range of Kaupapa Māori initiatives, including the MAI ki Tāmaki Facebook Group. I would also like to thank my sister Jenny Lee who continues to guide my work as an emerging researcher. Lastly, I would like to acknowledge my daughter Hine Pehia Lee-Hohaia and her many cousins, all of whom provide both a premise and a motivation for me engaging in this work of Kaupapa Māori research.

Writing this book has been a very collegial exercise and my first thanks go to my co-authors who have provided constant positive support throughout our research and writing processes. These amazing women have never failed to offer help and encouragement and it has been a privilege to work with them. Thanks to my co-researcher Inna for her vision and determination, Maryann for her wonderful insights and discussions, and Ann for her hard work and positivity. In addition, I would like to thank our proof readers and advisors Jane and Chris for their attention to detail and their patience with our shortcomings. Finally, a huge thanks to my family, my children Daniel and Camille, for always believing in me, making me dinner and intermittently helping clean the house, and my father Gordon, who sadly died this year, my mother Jill, and my sisters, Tina, Sandra and Chelle, for their support in all aspects of my life which made writing this book possible.

Chapter 1

Social Media in Tertiary Education:
Considerations and Potential Issues

Ann M. Simpson
Unitec Institute of Technology, New Zealand

Social media use is prevalent throughout the world and is now commonplace in higher education. The devices, support technologies, and social media applications used in higher education are in a constant state of change. Using social media in education creates new and sometimes challenging issues for institutions, instructors, and students. This chapter attempts to address some of the considerations and potential issues that impact our use of social media in the higher education classroom. It examines social media as an educational tool in higher education, possible pedagogies for social media use, potential educational contexts, and privacy concerns raised by social media use in educational environments. This chapter also provides a possible definition for social media and introduces some themes that will be explored in further detail in the following chapters.

INTRODUCTION

This introductory chapter introduces the potential for social media as an educational tool in higher education, possible pedagogies for social media use, potential educational contexts and privacy concerns raised by social media use in educational environments. Beginning with a brief account of the extensive current use of social media applications throughout the world, the chapter

DOI: 10.4018/978-1-5225-5826-2.ch001

discusses a variety of meanings for social media. Possible pedagogies for social media use are explored and potential educational contexts investigated. Some privacy concerns about the use of social media in educational environments are raised. This chapter also provides a possible definition for social media and introduces themes that will be explored in further detail in the following chapters. In addition, throughout this book, there are vignettes, case studies, or examples of how social media has been used in educational contexts which will assist in describing the content as well as providing potential examples for practitioners to experiment with.

BACKGROUND

Social media use around the world has increased at a phenomenal rate. The Global social media research summary, 2017 states that the number of Facebook active users alone stands at 1.8 billion users (Chaffey, 2017). At the time of writing, the total world population sits at 7.5 billion people (United Nations, 2017); this means that approximately 24% of the world's population is actively using Facebook daily (Chaffey, 2017). In addition, WhatsApp and Facebook Messenger and other popular social media platforms have approximately 1 billion active users each (Chaffey, 2017). Instagram has 600 million active users, Twitter has 317 million active users, and SnapChat and Skype both have 300 million active users respectively (Chaffey, 2017). WeChat and QQ, applications popular in China, have more than 850 million active users each (Chaffey, 2017). From the sheer volume and number of social media application users, it is undeniable that social media use is prevalent, worldwide, and will continue to grow. Although worldwide statistics on active student use of social media applications are not readily available, it is possible to surmise that many students' personal use of social media is included in those numbers. That is, some students will have experienced social media for personal use, business use, or both.

WHAT IS SOCIAL MEDIA?

At the core of social media is what Miller et al. call 'scalable sociality' (2016); two scales that describe the way in which people associate with each other to form social interactions or relations through social media (Miller et al., 2016). The first scale allows users to control the level of privacy for a group or audience "from the most private to the most public" (Miller et al., 2016, p. 3). The second scale allows users control over group size "from the smallest group to the largest group" (Miller et al., 2016, p. 3). These two scales can operate separately or together to determine the privacy and size of the group used for its purpose. They also describe the basic general function of social media applications and platforms in terms of the scope and size of the intended audience and how students can control and govern their audiences. Since the technologies utilized for social media will no doubt change in the future, the scales assist in describing the nature of social media regardless of the underlying technologies used in its creation. In terms of educational context, the scales can assist in describing and determining the size and scope of educational activity. They can also assist in the description of the difference between teacher- created, student-led and student self-created educational activities. While these scales assist in the description of what makes media social, they do not define it.

In many cases, social media is defined through example such as blogs, wikis, multi-media platforms and social networking sites (Selwyn, 2012; Tess, 2013). Social media enables collective user communities to generate, harness and share content for others (Selwyn, 2012). Defining social media is difficult because it changes constantly as the technologies that support it are changing (Tess, 2013). For the purposes of this book, social media is defined as any program or website that enables social interaction amongst an audience of users. The audience is determined by its users and the privacy of the content can be dictated by the collective users as well as the individuals.

THE EDUCATIONAL CONTEXT

Many students today have grown up knowing only a life of Wi-Fi connectivity and social media (Selwyn, 2012). For institutions and instructors alike, a drive exists to embrace these technologies to connect with students using the tools they are most likely to know and use (Selwyn, 2016). For example, many institutions now utilize social media to communicate with and recruit potential students (Hrastinski & Dennen, 2012). As these technologies change, the need for teaching and learning and pedagogical foundations in the use of these technologies will continue. Institutions, teachers and students will continue to connect, communicate and engage in educational activities and dialogues based on pedagogical foundations (Wegerif, 2007). As students continue to learn there will always be a need for them to discuss and connect with their

3

Table 1. Augmented reality and art? A true story

The following vignette describes how augmented reality incited the author's interest in social media for higher education.
One evening, my teenage daughter came up to me to show me her newest 'version' of herself. She showed me two photos she had taken of herself with her iPhone using Instagram; it applied a 'filter' over her image and she stated, "This is what I have to draw for my art class. What do you think? Which one, this one or the other one?"

Figure 1. Augmented reality: Filter 1	Figure 2. Augmented reality: Filter 2
	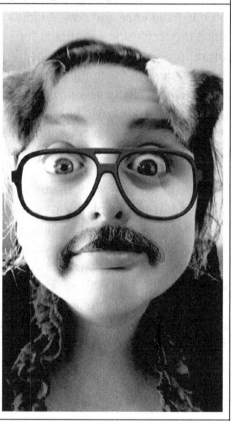
Source: A.M. Simpson	Source: A.M. Simpson

After laughing hysterically, I helped her choose one. I began to think how much her teenage years were different than mine because of social media. I found myself in astonishment that a social media tool, one designed to engage in interactive and social activities with others, was used for an art project. Even more interesting, was that this forced her to think about how she is portraying herself to her peers and teacher (her selected audience). This was an assigned task and not a self-generated one. While I use social media frequently, and not always in a classroom setting, I never thought it could be used for an art project in school. This experience started my personal quest for a better understanding of social media and how it could be applied through my work in the tertiary sector.

teachers, peers and others to facilitate their learning. It is the modalities of how students connect with others and the advance of affordances in web technologies that will continue to change.

Use of social media tools in everyday life is different from use in an educational context (Selwyn, 2012). Carr suggests that social media users in daily life seem to possess the ability to pick and choose snippets of knowledge to forward on to their social networks without developing a deeper knowledge or comprehension of that information (2010). If this is the case, how can this behavior be harnessed to engage students in educational activities? It is up to the teacher to determine how pedagogically-informed activities are designed and used to scaffold learning within the course and to guide the students through the appropriate use of the media for their activities. Some researchers, however, feel that this way of using social media in education is artificial and inherently flawed, as it reflects the traditional top-down teaching approach (Selwyn, 2012; Tess, 2013). For those researchers social media should be used from a grass roots, bottom-up approach in which content is generated by and for the students without instructor mandate.

The case study in Table 2 describes how an instructor implemented Blogging as a research tool for students in her class.

Blended Learning

Blended learning (BL) provides opportunities for increased interaction amongst students and teachers, flexibility in the environments used and potential for increased student engagement (Vaughan, 2007). Blended learning is defined as the combination of the digital and physical classroom environments; digital environments can include the use of a learning management system such as Moodle in combination with other digital tools such as social media. The physical environments involve the physical spaces that the face to face sessions are conducted in. The 2017 New Media Consortium report on Technology in Higher Education notes that the inclusion of BL in tertiary institutions is a currently a high priority for many academic institutions internationally (Jaramillo, 2017; Spring, Graham, & Hadlock, 2017). Social media has increased opportunities for students in blended learning environments and has allowed a shift from the traditional top down approach to student-centered learning. That is learning that is generated by the students themselves to share with each other through collaborative discourse and interaction via social media.

5

Table 2. Case study: Blog as a research tool

"To show that research had been done over a period of time and had been thought about by students"
The lecturer wanted a place for students to accumulate and collate their research over a period of time. She felt that many students were conducting cursory research at the last minute and spending little time critically examining their research issue. By collecting a variety of material over several weeks the lecturer hoped that students would research in more depth and have more time to critically evaluate their material.
To encourage this collection of resource material over a period of time, the lecturer added blog posting as an assessment item. For this, students were marked on the number of their posts and given top marks for this item if they posted every day. To encourage variety another item measured diversity of posts and students were encouraged to find a wide range of material that related to their research topic.
"(they had to) post every day for a month. A variety: from academic to general websites, newspapers, position papers, government websites, academic journal articles, magazines, podcasts, cartoons, music, photos, self-made -own videos, observations and personal reflections. This led to judgements, personal reflection".
The lecturer was also interested in giving the students a voice and privileging their knowledge, and encouraging both formal and informal postings, allowing students to discuss their knowledge and point of view. In addition, she wanted the students to be "seduced into enjoying their work" and to discover that the more their effort the better their final product.
Students were able to like each other's posts but, as there was no comment function available with Tumblr, Pinterest, and blogs, others couldn't comment on posts unless they imported the post to their own page. The lecturer felt that students had to think about what they wrote as they had to own anything they re-blogged onto their own page. She also thought this reduced the negativity experienced on some social media. 'Likes' also meant students experienced positive reinforcement only from each other, creating a positive group atmosphere.
This blogging achieved the goal of more and deeper research, more in depth consideration of that research, improved students' presentation content and seemed to increase engagement.
"(Students) enjoyed using it and usually made over 30 posts …seeing students really engage, a nice buzz. (it was) student directed, the lecturer scaffolds. It was a great low stakes/ early reward assessment for early in the course."

The rise of social media use in higher education has led to a dramatic shift away from conventional classroom-based learning (Adams Becker, Cummins, et al., 2017). There has been a growth in interest towards student-centered pedagogy and the role of students in course design, content generation and delivery. The broad conceptualization of student-centered pedagogy holds that teaching strategies adhere to "a participatory mode of decision-making in all aspects of learning" and focus on "uncovering the excitement in intellectual and emotional discovery" (Motschnig-Pitrik & Holzinger, 2002, p. 162). Student-centered pedagogy, then, appears to describe learning and teaching in social media settings. Hoffman and Novak state that student-centered pedagogy enables its users to "…connect, create, consume, and control", key elements in social media use (2011, p. 5). Social media can provide educators with specific social contexts and resources that "exist outside the formal spaces of the institution" creating "opportunities for authentic learning that is personally meaningful and relevant" (McLoughlin & Lee, 2010, p. 31). What must be considered is that social media can potentially reinforce student-centered teaching practices by presenting alternative ways to knowledge acquisition and giving students more power and control over their learning.

Changing Learning Environments

Traditional lecture style classrooms across the world are slowly being replaced with modern innovative spaces. A modern innovative learning space is one that contains moveable and configurable seating arrangements, equipment and sometimes partitions or walls. For example, a modern innovative learning space can involve moveable computers that display on large screens alongside moveable, modular desks that can be clustered together to form groups or separated for individual work. The classroom space design and resources available within reconfigured learning spaces can potentially change the way teachers and students interact and engage in their teaching and learning. Research suggests that the ways in which students interact with each other using the tools available to them, both digital and physical, can potentially impact how they learn (Carvalho, Goodyear, & de Laat, 2017). That is, a modern learning space can change the way the students and instructor engage in learning activities and dialogues based on their proximity, the social aspects of their in-class relationships and the resources they use in the classroom, with potential for improved learning (Goodyear, Carvalho, & Dohn, 2016; Ravelli & McMurtrie, 2016). Social media and other technologies can be mobile and can be utilized across the digital and physical classroom spaces and can provide significant opportunities for learning activities.

In the past 12 years, blended learning environments have been contextualized and described as learning networks (Goodyear, 2005; Yeoman, 2015). A learning network, as the word network implies, focuses on the connections of things and people in a learning environment (Thibaut, Curwood, Carvalho, & Simpson, 2015). The 'things' in a learning environment, sometimes referred to artefacts, can be either digital or physical and consist of anything that is utilized for learning purposes such as whiteboards, learning management systems like Moodle, handouts, books and social media tools. The people in a learning network consist of the students, instructors, or other individuals (guest speakers or librarians, for example) who participate in the learning network. A learning network is defined as "…a heterogeneous assemblage of people and things connected in activities that have learning as an explicit goal or as a significant side effect" (Goodyear et al., 2016, p. 93). Learning and activities in the learning network are "… mediated across agents, tools, and spaces" (Thibaut et al., 2015, p. 459). That is, learning activities occur through the connections of the people involved, the things or artefacts they use to assist in learning and the digital and physical spaces in which learning can occur. For example, the social media tools such as Facebook or Twitter, can be viewed and utilized as tools to provide connection and networking opportunities for students and others in a learning network. In this instance, social media can play a role in learning networks.

Real-world learning is becoming more important to students as they obtain qualifications to become job ready in both vocational and higher education settings (Adams Becker et al., 2017). Real-world learning fosters connections between what they are learning and the real-world experience. Of benefit in trades or vocational training is the use of e-portfolios utilizing a wide of array of technologies including, social media tools, digital photos, videos, and recordings and links to resources to document skills or tasks. Nore (2015) found students could document their skills and tasks through creating videos with their devices while on site at work and share them for assessment and skills evidence for potential employers. In this case, Nore created a learning environment that enabled the extension of the learning into the students' work environments.

Cochrane, Narayan and Oldfield, in their study on authentic contexts of mobile social media use in New Zealand, analyzed three case studies from three different institutions in New Zealand (2014). Each case study was implemented with the same methodology informed by nine authentic learning principles (Cochrane et al., 2014). They include "…real-life, authentic tasks, access to expert performances and modelling processes, multiples roles and perspectives, construction of knowledge, reflection, articulation, coaching and scaffolding, and authentic assessment" (Cochrane et al., 2014, pp. 127–128). 'Authentic context and tasks' refers to how the learning or knowledge gained will be used in life or work, for example using a lathe in a construction workshop. 'Access to expert performances or modelling processes' describes how students can be shown how social media, if relevant, is used in their targeted work environment such as Xero for on-site invoicing for a tradesperson, as well to potentially video or post images of learning or task achievements, such as a kitchen installation (Cochrane et al., 2014, pp. 127–128). In addition, 'Multiple roles and perspectives' means that students are able to construct knowledge and content across 'formal and informal' learning contexts relevant to their authentic learning contexts (Cochrane et al., 2014, pp. 127–128). 'Collaborative construction of knowledge' refers to the fact that the students and instructors as well as any others involved in the students learning can collaborate and co-construct knowledge together, such as user forums (Cochrane et al., 2014, pp. 127–128). 'Reflection' refers to the self-reflective opportunities potentially present in the authentic context and social media tools can provide a potential modality for this expression such as blogging or keeping a diary (Cochrane et al., 2014, pp. 127–128). 'Articulation' refers to the different modalities of presentation that can be utilized with mobile social media, for example links to Piktochart or Prezi, infographics presentation tools in an authentic learning context (Cochrane et al., 2014, pp. 127–128). 'Coaching and scaffolding' provides opportunities for students to teach and learn from each other, their instructors, and anyone from their social learning communities (Cochrane et al., 2014, pp. 127–128). Finally, 'authentic assessment' describes that the assessment activities created should utilize the affordances of the mobile technologies available, such as taking a formative quiz through Kahoot, an online interactive quiz tool (Cochrane et al., 2014, pp. 127–128).

These nine principles can act as a useful guide to assist in the generation of authentic contexts in which social media can be used. Authentic contexts and use of social media and in many cases the potential mobile devices and their affordances can facilitate more opportunities for students to engage in their learning networks. Research into social media and its use in blended learning environments, learning networks and authentic environments will need to continue, since the technologies constantly change, students' requirements change, and teaching and work environments change.

Digital Divide

With the advancement of mobile devices, learning can take place in a mobile way. As Parsons suggests, mobile learning is an extension of e-learning and distance learning and offers additional affordances through the newer mobile technologies, such as learning in specific contexts, creating shared resources, the affordances of Web 2.0 technologies, and more opportunities for student self-ownership of learning (2014). While the potentials of the technologies are considerable, there remains a gap for the few who do not have access or skills required to use the technologies. Wei, Teo, Chan, and Tan suggest there are three potential digital divides: access to digital technologies, the capability of using digital technologies, and the outcomes based on the capabilities of the individuals using the technologies (2011). In terms of access to technologies, the ECAR study of Undergraduate Students and Information Technology 2016 report surveyed 71,641 students from 183 countries and 37 U.S. states on undergraduates' use and access to information technology in tertiary education (Brooks, 2016). The research found that over half of students surveyed owned one of each of the three major pieces of device technology, including a laptop, a tablet and a smartphone (Brooks, 2016). The study found despite the high rates of device ownership that 1% of students did not own any (Brooks, 2016). This showed that technology access for some students continues to remain an issue around the world (Brooks, 2016; Selwyn, 2012, 2016). However, to assist this issue, many institutions offer loan computers or computer labs as well as software and IT skills training support to minimize disadvantage to those that do not have access (Wei et al., 2011).

Aside from personal device ownership, another potential barrier for students is lack of access to the Internet. The 2016 UNESCO's Annual World Education Report suggests that internet access is not always readily available in developing countries and is largely dependent upon a combination of factors, including the institution's geographic location, ability to pay for internet access, and the country's telecom infrastructure (2016). For example, in 2012, the Mongolian government provided funding to their schools to ensure Internet connectivity continued to be available to students regardless of the cost (Unesco, 2016). For both developed and developing nations, the digital divide continues to be an issue for some students and must not be discounted at the government, institutional and course levels (Adams Becker et al., 2017; Brooks, 2016; Unesco, 2016). Institutions and instructors should continue to provide alternative modes of access and training for students to provide equal opportunities for device access and digital literacy in social media use.

International Students and Cultural Inclusivity

Many attempts in current research have been made to identify specific possibilities of social media for international education and culturally relevant practices. The questions have been asked with regard to social media use in learning and teaching of international students. Concerning challenges associated with study abroad, the research has been focusing on the extent to which social media may help students to overcome cultural and academic differences. For example, with regard to the role of social media in supporting international students' adjustment to new educational and social environments, some researchers highlight that it has a "positive effect on students" grades, engagement and motivation" (Saw, Abbott & Donaghey, 2013, p. 3). In the same vein, Lin, Peng, Kim, Kim and LaRose (2012) found that social networking sites contribute to international students' "online bridging capital and social adjustments" (p. 436). In the Australian Journal of Educational technology, McCarthy reports on results of a two-year study on the use of Facebook in combination with face to face lectures and tutorials that involved not only local, but international students. The author holds the view that "the blending of real and virtual environments increased peer interaction and academic engagement" and enhanced students' first year experience overall (McCarthy, 2010, p. 738).

Another aspect is the growing prominence of the effectiveness of social media within a cross-cultural educational context. Although there are no universally accepted teaching practices specifically designed for the international classroom integrating social media, some researchers have defined principles of pedagogy for online learning environments. For instance, McLoughlin (2006) states that to effectively teach in cross-cultural online settings there is a need for culturally inclusive pedagogy and curriculum that "are flexible, adaptable and relevant to students from a diverse range of cultural and language backgrounds" (p. 7). In response to the continuing internationalization of tertiary education, there seems to be one reasonable clear-cut approach to ensure quality in the international classroom – to create learning experiences for international students that are responsive to their personal learning needs and goals, and allow to showcase their existing skills and knowledge. In this respect, social media can potentially serve as a tool to support and enhance learning experiences for students, more specifically international ones.

Privacy Anyone?

Today, many higher education institutions use learning management systems to create and govern their online courses. One of the many advantages of learning management systems is that they usually offer a myriad of social media tools for students and staff to use in their courses. LMSs' are usually self-contained within their institutional networks and can insure privacy of student information and data. Social media applications, on the other hand, are controlled and governed by corporate entities, thus creating privacy concerns for students. Should therefore an academic institution prevent students from utilizing social media software programs due to privacy issues?

Commercial social media sites are backed by incredible amounts of corporate investment and because they are businesses they seek ways to continue to increase profits. One way they accomplish this is through selling user information. As soon as an individual signs up for 'free' access to a commercially driven social media site, the individual agrees to the site's' terms and conditions; this means, in many cases, the individual has potentially forfeited his or her personal information for the corporation to resell to others (Jacobsson, 2010). In addition, the individual has given permission to the corporation to monitor his or her onsite behavior for the purposes of targeted marketing (DeMers, 2017). For example, if an individual looked up traveling to Thailand on Facebook, a mathematical formula, an algorithm, will be activated and advertisements on traveling to Thailand will 'suddenly' display on the user's Facebook homepage or 'feed'. Based on how students utilize Facebook in class, content will be served to the students through Facebook advertisers. The institution and the instructor do not have control over the advertising content. For some researchers, the commercial presence in commercial social media sites negatively impacts the sites' potential affordances for learning and teaching (Friesen & Lowe, 2012).

Alternatively, non-commercial social media sites, ones that do not feature in Global Social Media Statistics Summary, usually consist of user- created and monitored content (Zheng, Niiya, & Warschauer, 2015). Non-commercial sites do not resell an individual's information. They do not have the financial backing that corporate giants do to attract and maintain the number of individual users that commercialized sites can. In some cases, this can mean limited program functionality when compared to the commercialized sites. When asking students to use commercial social media websites, we must inform them about threats to their personal information when we endeavor to engage them in using social media applications and activities. Institutions, instructors and students should inform students of what happens with their personal information when they utilize corporate social media sites, so they can make informed choices about their participation in educational social media activities.

Another potential concern is how other users in the social media community disseminate content. Cain and Fink illustrate this through the metaphor of email (Cain & Fink III, 2010). Emails, like letters, are private until opened or viewed (Cain & Fink III, 2010). Once the email is opened it is up to the discretion of the recipient to choose how he or she utilizes the information. That is, once social media content has been posted or viewed, the audience or individual chooses how to engage with the content afterward; this typically includes copying and pasting or re-sharing the content with others (Cain & Fink III, 2010). In many instances, students will have pre-existing accounts, for example on Facebook, that contain highly private information which is deemed personal and not appropriate for a classroom page. How students portray themselves in social media sites forms another potential concern. It is suggested that for educational purposes students create a generic account for their educational persona. Or as described in further detail in Chapters 3 and 4 of this book, students can watch and learn what appropriate protocols and behavior are according to the culture of the form. Alternatively, and perhaps most optimal, let the class decide the rules of appropriate behavior in the digital space, in digital citizenship, in the classroom and how they will conduct themselves in this shared collaborative group environment as suggested in Chapters 2 and 5. It is extremely important for institutions, teachers and students to work together to establish guidelines and rules around online behavior, privacy and the ethical practice and use of content dissemination of social media in the educational context.

FUTURE RESEARCH DIRECTIONS

While a phenomenal amount of research already exists into the social media landscape and how it is currently being utilized in higher education, further research is warranted to gain a better understanding on how the technologies impact institutional responsibilities in terms of student information and privacy as well as instructor and student support. The digital support structures that enable access to the Internet and social media technologies will continue to open possibilities for social interaction and potential learning opportunities. Further research into the international classroom and cultural contexts for students and classes continues to be needed. While blended learning seems to be gaining wider acceptance and adoption, further research into blended learning that focuses on the new technological affordances and tools is warranted. Also, further research into learning networks could provide more clarity on social media use in the digital and physical spaces of modern or refurbished learning environments and how it impacts the students and teachers involved in terms of the learning opportunities, tools utilized and the artefacts created.

CONCLUSION

The increase in technological advances in software, devices and infrastructures impact opportunities for learning networks, the changing nature of the learning environments and potential learning opportunities for students to engage with.

Social media is part of daily life for many students worldwide and there are many potential opportunities to embrace it in the higher education. Because of this fact, cultural contexts and sensitivity should be considered for students who choose to obtain their education outside of their home countries. While device use and access is increasing and common place for many students, for others the digital divide continues to remain an important issue in terms of access, skillset and outcomes. In addition, privacy issues continue to be a concern for institutions, instructors and students alike. However, the opportunities for social collaborative learning are enormous and research in this area must continue to explore its potential, despite the challenges for students and social media use in higher education.

As the ancient Greek philosopher Heraclitus taught his students, the only constant in life is change (Kirk, 1951). This constant state of change aptly describes the state of social media use in higher education today. This book covers a relevant, in the moment view of the state of social media use in various contexts used in New Zealand. The following chapters address a series of pedagogical concepts related to students in the international classroom, culturally relevant practices of social media, teachers' experiences with social media implementation in the tertiary environment, and emergent social media trends and possibilities for higher education. It is hoped that it will provide further understanding about the dynamic nature of social media use and provide examples and ideas for potential implementation.

REFERENCES

Adams Becker, S., Cumins, M., Davis, A., Freeman, A., Hall Giesinger, C., & Ananthanarayanan, V. (2017). *NMC horizon report: 2017 higher education edition* (p. 60). Austin, TX: The New Media Consortium. Retrieved from http://cdn.nmc.org/media/2017-nmc-horizon-report-he-EN.pdf

Brooks, D. C. (2016). *ECAR study of undergraduate students and information technology*. Retrieved from https://library.educause.edu/resources/2016/6/~/media/files/library/2016/10/ers1605.pdf

Cain, J., & Fink, J. L. III. (2010). Legal and ethical issues regarding social media and pharmacy education. *American Journal of Pharmaceutical Education*, 74(10), 1–8. doi:10.5688/aj7410184 PMID:21436925

Carr, N. (2010). The web shatters focus, rewires brains. *Wired.Com, 24.* Retrieved from http://aplangandcomp.blogs.rsu1.org/files/2010/06/the-shallows.pdf

Carvalho, L., Goodyear, P., & de Laat, M. (Eds.). (2017). *Place-based spaces for networked learning.* New York: Routledge, Taylor and Francis Group. Retrieved from http://ezproxy.massey.ac.nz/login?url=http://massey.eblib.com.au/patron/FullRecord.aspx?p=4579047

Chaffey, D. (2017, April 27). *Global social media statistics summary 2017.* Retrieved September 14, 2017, from http://www.smartinsights.com/social-media-marketing/social-media-strategy/new-global-social-media-research/

Cochrane, T., Narayan, V., & Oldfield, J. (2014). 11 emerging technologies in New Zealand. In Activity Theory, Authentic Learning and Emerging Technologies: Towards a Transformative Higher Education Pedagogy (pp. 126–143). Academic Press.

DeMers, J. (2017, January 23). *Does your social media app know too much about you?* Retrieved October 26, 2017, from https://www.forbes.com/sites/jaysondemers/2017/01/23/does-your-social-media-app-know-too-much-about-you/

Friesen, N., & Lowe, S. (2012). The questionable promise of social media for education: Connective learning and the commercial imperative. *Journal of Computer Assisted Learning, 28*(3), 183–194. doi:10.1111/j.1365-2729.2011.00426.x

Goodyear, P. (2005). Educational design and networked learning: Patterns, pattern languages and design practice. *Australasian Journal of Educational Technology, 21*(1), 82–101. doi:10.14742/ajet.1344

Goodyear, P., Carvalho, L., & Dohn, N. B. (2016). Artefacts and Activities in the Analysis of Learning Networks. In *Research, Boundaries, and Policy in Networked Learning* (pp. 93–110). Cham: Springer. doi:10.1007/978-3-319-31130-2_6

Hew, K. F., & Cheung, W. S. (2013). Use of Web 2.0 technologies in K-12 and higher education: The search for evidence-based practice. *Educational Research Review, 9,* 47–64. doi:10.1016/j.edurev.2012.08.001

Hoffman, D. L., & Novak, T. P. (2011). Marketing communication in digital era. *Marketing Management*, *20*(3), 36–43.

Hrastinski, S., & Dennen, V. (2012). Social media in higher education: Introduction to the special issue. *The Internet and Higher Education*, *15*(1), 1–2. doi:10.1016/j.iheduc.2011.11.004

Jacobsson, S. (2010, May 20). *Social networking sites may be sharing your info with advertisers*. Retrieved October 26, 2017, from https://www.pcworld.com/article/196869/Social_Network_Privacy.html

Jaramillo, S. G. (2017). Horizon Report-2017 Higher Education Edition. *CUADERNO ACTIVA*, *9*(9), 171.

Kirk, G. S. (1951). Natural Change in Heraclitus. Oxford University Press.

Lin, J.-H., Peng, W., Kim, M., Kim, S. Y., & LaRose, R. (2012). Social networking and adjustments among international students. *New Media & Society*, *14*(3), 421–440.

McCarthy, J. (2010). Blended learning environments: Using social networking sites to enhance the first year experience. *Australasian Journal of Educational Technology*, *26*(6), 729–740.

McLoughlin, C. (2006). Inclusivity and alignment: Principles of pedagogy, task and assessment design for effective cross-cultural online learning. *Distance Education*, *22*(1), 7–29. doi:10.1080/0158791010220102

McLoughlin, C., & Lee, M. J. W. (2010). Personalised and self-regulated learning in the Web 2.0 era: International exemplars of innovative pedagogy using social software. *Australasian Journal of Educational Technology*, *26*(1). doi:10.14742/ajet.1100

Miller, D., Costa, E., Haynes, N., McDonald, T., Nicolescu, R., Sinanan, J., … Wang, X. (Eds.). (2016). What is social media? In *How the World Changed Social Media* (Vol. 1, pp. 1–8). UCL Press. Retrieved from http://www.jstor.org/stable/j.ctt1g69z35.8

Motschnig-Pitrik, R., & Holzinger, A. (2002). Student-centered teaching meets new media: Concept and case study. *Journal of Educational Technology & Society*, *5*(4), 160–172.

Parsons, D. (2014). The future of mobile learning and implications for education and training. In *Increasing access through mobile learning* (Vol. 217, pp. 217–229). Vancouver, Canada: Commonwealth of Learning (COL); Athabasca University. Retrieved from http://oasis.col.org/bitstream/handle/11599/558/pub_Mobile%20Learning_web.pdf#page=234

Ravelli, L. J., & McMurtrie, R. J. (2016). Networked places as communicative resources. *Place-Based Spaces for Networked Learning*, 111–130.

Saw, G., Abbott, W., & Donaghey, J. (2013). *Social media for international students – it's not all about Facebook.* Library Management. Retrieved from http://epublications.bond.edu.au/library_pubs/35

Selwyn, N. (2012). Social Media in Higher Education. *The Europa World of Learning*, 1–10.

Selwyn, N. (2016). Digital downsides: Exploring university students' negative engagements with digital technology. *Teaching in Higher Education*, 1–16. doi:10.1080/13562517.2016.1213229

Spring, K. J., Graham, C. R., & Hadlock, C. A. (2017). The current landscape of international blended learning. *International Journal of Technology Enhanced Learning*, *8*(1), 84–102. doi:10.1504/IJTEL.2016.075961

Tess, P. A. (2013). The role of social media in higher education classes (real and virtual) – A literature review. *Computers in Human Behavior*, *29*(5), A60–A68. doi:10.1016/j.chb.2012.12.032

Thibaut, P., Curwood, J. S., Carvalho, L., & Simpson, A. (2015). Moving across physical and online spaces: A case study in a blended primary classroom. *Learning, Media and Technology*, *40*(4), 458–479. doi:10.1080/17439884.2014.959971

UNESCO. (Ed.). (2016). *Education for people and planet: creating sustainable futures for all* (2nd ed.). Paris: UNESCO.

United Nations. (2017). *World population prospects: The 2017 revision, key findings and advance tables* (No. ESA/P/WP/248). Retrieved from https://esa.un.org/unpd/wpp/Publications/Files/WPP2017_KeyFindings.pdf

Vaughan, N. (2007). Perspectives on blended learning in higher education. *International Journal on E-Learning*, *6*(1), 81–94.

Wegerif, R. (2007). *Dialogic, Education and Technology: Expanding the space of learning* (Vol. 7). Exeter, UK: Springer Science & Business Media. doi:10.1007/978-0-387-71142-3

Wei, K.-K., Teo, H.-H., Chan, H. C., & Tan, B. C. Y. (2011). Conceptualizing and testing a social cognitive model of the digital divide. *Information Systems Research, 22*(1), 170–187. doi:10.1287/isre.1090.0273

Yeoman, P. (2015, October 28). *Habits and habitats: An ethnography of learning entanglement.* The University of Sydney, Australia. Retrieved from http://trove.nla.gov.au/work/199277646?q=pippa+yeoman&c=book&versionId=218342152

Zheng, B., Niiya, M., & Warschauer, M. (2015). Wikis and collaborative learning in higher education. *Technology, Pedagogy and Education, 24*(3), 357–374. doi:10.1080/1475939X.2014.948041

KEY TERMS AND DEFINITIONS

Authentic Learning Principles: Authentic, real, life-like learning is based upon the following nine principles: real-life, authentic tasks, access to expert performances and modelling processes, multiples roles and perspectives, construction of knowledge, reflection, articulation, coaching and scaffolding, and authentic assessment.

Blended Learning: Described as the combination of the digital and physical classroom environments, digital environments can include the use of a learning management system such as Moodle in combination with other digital tools such as social media.

Digital Divide: Described as a skills gap for the students who do not have access to or the skills required to use technologies.

Digital Privacy: A term used to describe the privacy of an individual's information through the social media tools used. Privacy is determined by the scalable sociality (defined above) set by the individual.

Learning Networks: A connected network of agents (students, teachers, and other individuals), tools (artefacts, blogs, whiteboards, Facebook pages, wikis, etc.), and spaces (both physical classroom spaces and digital spaces) who use the network for a learning purpose.

Modern Learning Environments or Spaces: A learning environment or space that contains moveable and configurable seating arrangements, equipment, and sometimes partitions or walls.

Real-World Learning: Learning that occurs in real-life contexts, such as a construction apprentice learning on the job at a building site.

Scalable Sociality: Two scales that describe the nature of the way in which people associate with each other to form social interactions or relations available through social media. The first scale describes privacy control from private to public and the second scale describes the size of the audience from the smallest group to the largest group.

Social Media: Any program or website that enables social interaction amongst an audience of users. The audience is determined by its users and the privacy of the content can be dictated by the collective users as well as the individuals.

Chapter 2
Facebook in the International Classroom

Inna Piven
Unitec Institute of Technology, New Zealand

ABSTRACT

The case explores international students' learning experiences with Facebook-based activities within the eight-week study term known as the intensive mode of course delivery. By implementing participant observation and two asynchronous Facebook focus groups, the study investigates the potential values of Facebook for learning from international students' perspective. In addition, the case looks at the challenges faced by students and discusses key factors that may impact international students' experiences with courses that incorporate Facebook as a learning tool. The research is framed in the context of New Zealand tertiary education and intended as a contribution to the emerging body of educational research on social media.

INTRODUCTION

The world that is fast emerging from the clash of new values and technologies, new life-styles and modes of communication, demands wholly new ideas and concepts. (Toffler, 1980, p. 2)

During the last decade there has been a noticeable interest among educators towards social media and the changes they have brought about to teaching and learning. For many universities and institutions, emerging online learning

DOI: 10.4018/978-1-5225-5826-2.ch002

environment is a novel situation. Matters are complicated further by the fact that tertiary student profiles, demands of the employment market as well as the learners' expectations, personal goals, learning habits and behavior have also changed. In addition, taking into consideration a constantly growing number of international students coming to New Zealand, tertiary education authorities have pointed out a necessity to develop new models of course delivery with a strong focus on communication and social connections.

Given the above issues, the concern here is to explore not just new social contexts for learning that tertiary educators suddenly have been provided with, but first and foremost learners' experiences with these contexts. Although teachers and learning designers have been using social media in course design and delivery for a while, academic researchers have only recently begun to acknowledge the importance of looking at social media in the tertiary education context.

In this regard, research questions, typically, have ranged from affordances of social media in contract with learning management systems, to social media for students' self-regulated leaning, and teachers' views on benefits and challenges associated with social media. Absent in current research are insights into international learners' experiences with social media. As has already been mentioned, due to the internationalization of tertiary education, there is a need for new, well-functioning models that could respond to "the demands of more diverse learners", and a "changing society" (New Zealand Productivity Commission, 2017). The motivation behind this study is informed by several gaps identified through the literature review as set out below.

Firstly, the literature review reveals that there is a lack of empirical data and evidence related to international students' learning experiences with social media as a learning tool, specifically in the context of intensive courses that are defined as "compressed, concentrated, or short-term learning" (Serdyukov, 2008, p. 37). Secondly, despite the growing use of social media in delivering courses, the research into what kind of factors may impact students' learning experiences remains limited. Finally, the existing research still focuses on a homogeneous rather than diverse student population, suggesting that insights are required into international students' learning experiences with social media.

This study aims at exploring international students' learning experiences with Facebook-based activities incorporated in two undergraduate intensive business courses: Event Planning and Management and Entrepreneurship at Otago Polytechnic Auckland International Campus, New Zealand (OPAIC).

Therefore, the research question is: What are the educational values of Facebook for international students enrolled in the intensive courses?

The study has been guided by the following supporting questions:

1. What are international students' views on the intensive courses that incorporate Facebook closed groups as a learning tool?
2. What are international students' views on Facebook as a learning tool in comparison with learning management systems such as Moodle?
3. What are the factors that may impact international students' learning experiences with courses incorporating Facebook?

The chapter starts with a theoretical background by looking at some key questions and concepts associated with social media, international students' experiences, and the intensive mode of course delivery. It also details the gaps in the existing research and explains the research methodology and design. Drawing on research data, the next section discusses international students' learning experiences with Facebook. The chapter concludes with solutions and recommendations followed by an outline of prospects for future research.

BACKGROUND

For nearly a decade, there has been a growing interest towards social media in educational research that covers a wide range of topics from practical issues of knowledge sharing to risks linked to online learning environments. To develop a more strategic view on social media use in education, it is important to work through some key definitions and useful concepts related to social media.

Kaplan and Haenlein (2010) argue that "there is no systematic way in which different social media applications can be categorized" (Kaplan & Haenlein, 2010, p. 61). However, some forms of social media have been identified based on its core activities and the degree of the user's social presence. Hence, scholars recognize that social media include different types of online applications, for example social networks or social media (Facebook and Twitter), blogs, virtual game communities (the Second Life), and content communities, such as Wikipedia and YouTube.

Research by Hoffman and Novak (2011) states that social media allows users to be orientated toward "higher-order goals: connect, create, consume and control" (p. 4). Beer and Burrows (2010) add to that understanding, highlighting the participatory culture of social media. In a similar vein, Fischer and Reuber (2010, p. 5), using the example of Twitter, state "social media appears to be giving rise to new types of social interactions". This is also a central argument in Shao's study, which suggests that social media is useful for different social activities, including "participation in social interaction and community development" (as cited in Heinonen, 2011, p. 358). Heinrichs, Lim and Lim (2011) believe that social media is "an interaction tool used by individuals to discover and share content, opinions, and information" (p. 347). Overall, scholars tend to view social media as: a) a computer-generated environment; b) real time online communications; c) media for collaboration, group activities and sharing; and d) user-generated content.

Even though the advent of social media has prompted a significant amount of new research in the educational context, the studies on social media use in the international classroom are limited. Meanwhile conventional modes of course design, content areas, and learning and teaching models are continuously being challenged due to an increased number of international students (Ho & Piven, 2015). According to the New Zealand Productivity Commission Report (2017), "in contrast to domestic students, the number of international students enrolled with New Zealand tertiary providers has steadily increased" (p.36). Available data on enrolments in New Zealand tertiary education shows that "international students made up to 15 percent of all tertiary education students in 2015, up from 13 percent in 2014" (International students enrolled in tertiary education, 2017). Moreover, a new high has been predicted for 2018 due to students coming from China and Latin America (Gerritsen, 2017).

In scholarly discussions about international students' experiences, some of the following topics typically rise to the surface:

- There are many challenges faced by international students that are linked to unfamiliar pedagogy and teaching practices. As Sherry, Thomas and Hong Chui (2010) point out "problems may occur in adjusting to a new culture [in terms of] experiencing academic difference" (p. 34). Taking into consideration the diversity of international students, it is important to explore if social media can help students from different cultural backgrounds to adapt to a new learning environment.
- It has been suggested that social media can serve as a social support mechanism for international students' cultural adaptation (Ryan, Magro & Sharp, 2011). However, the conclusions presented in research around this topic are mainly literature based and lack empirical evidence.

- The term "international student experience has now become a catch-all phrase", and "has almost lost its meaning and direction" (Welikala, 2015). While universities put a lot of effort into understanding the key factors that may affect international students' learning, the discussion is still limited to cultural differences or differences in learning styles.

- There is no common understanding of the alternative ways of learning or of how to make effective use of new technologies including social media "to address the unique needs of international students" and not to "leave these students feeling disappointed, unfulfilled, and even exploited" (Sherry, Thomas & Chui, 2010, p. 34).

In general, researchers and educators recognize that international students have to "deal with academic challenges, social isolation, and cultural adjustment" (Wu, Garza & Guzman, 2014, p. 1). Over the years, it has become clear that "the tertiary education system is not well-placed to respond to uncertain future trends and demands of more diverse learners" (New Zealand Productivity Commission Report, 2017) and new strategies responsive to a changing student profile are much needed.

The changing student profile can be seen in relation not only to internalization of tertiary education, but also to ongoing technological developments. A report "The social revolution" by Hootsuite, a well-known platform for managing social media, describes today's students as "truly digital natives" (2017). Baird and Fisher (2006) characterized the new generation of learners as "always-on", and as those who "expect to utilize technology in their learning" and connect "to their peers, professors, and course content through… social networks…" (p. 10). Interestingly enough, despite a variety of learning management systems currently available for educators, such as Moodle, Echo360, Blackboard, there has been a noticeable gravitation towards social media. It seems that pressure on tertiary education providers to meet new situations signalled by both a "changing society and world of work" ("New Zealand Productivity Commission Report", 2017) has become stronger and stronger. However, according to Hootsuite's report based on the analysis of 128 Australian universities and institutions, tertiary education has been "struggling with the transition to digital campuses, where social media has the potential to connect and deliver a revolutionized student experience" (Hootsuite, 2017).

Understanding the challenges and barriers to international students' learning, a project "The International Student Experience" undertaken by Education New Zealand and Study Auckland pointed to a need to design courses that are "student-centered", "focus beyond the on-campus experience", and enable students "[to] grow as individuals" ("Journey to transformational student experience", 2017). The project has put forward a strategy that aims at creating "the ecosystem surrounding international students" based on collaboration, social connectivity and communication ("International Student Experience Project", 2017). Trying to redress the situation faced by international students, some scholars have been emphasizing the importance of Facebook-like channels in constructing the institution-learner relationships. According to Roblyer, McDaniel, Webb, Herman and Witty (2010), "faculty who see teaching as establishing a relationship with students may view [deploying] Facebook-like technologies as an efficient, even business-like way to accomplish that connection" (p. 135). Ryan, Magro and Sharp (2011), in their study on first semester international Ph.D. students, have carefully analyzed the impact of Facebook groups on students' adaptation to a Ph.D. program and a new culture. They have come to the conclusion that the social network enabled "various types of knowledge exchange" and helped "students alleviate apprehension by the sharing of a variety of experiences" (p. 13). According to Sleeman, Lang and Lemon (2016), "social media facilitates important communication, acculturation, and educational [process] and "can assist educators in developing more inclusive learning environments" (p. 402). Similarly, Zhao (2016) sets educational providers the task of embracing the accessibility of social media to "maintain connection with international students beyond the classroom to offer better support for students in their everyday lives" (p. 6).

While some educators agree that social media can positively contribute to students' learning, others think that using social media "is as much of a challenge for many students as it may be for most educators" (Gray, Lucas, & Kennedy, 2010, p. 971). Very interesting insights into social media use in the international classroom have been introduced by Alfarhoud, Alahmad, Alqahtani and Alhassan (2016). Their findings reveal that "many international students see that using social media during the class is a distraction factor..." Having said that, the authors retain the belief that social media offers very helpful tools if they are well integrated with the learning environment.

In addition, research publications draw attention to the educational potential of social media. It has been established that social media can effectively be used for learning purposes. For example, Lofgren suggested "social media in education settings has a positive impact on students' comprehension of class material" (as cited in Alfarhoud et al., 2016, p. 45). A New Zealand based study by Rahman (2014) concludes that social media should not only be allowed in class, but also be actively integrated in academic programs as international students can then use them for independent learning.

To meet "the global context of education" and "the character and composition of students" (Davies, 2006, p. 1) some tertiary education providers have been offering intensive courses characterized as "semester- or quarter-equivalent classes offered in compressed, accelerated, or condensed formats" in which the number of weeks per semester is reduced while the number of hours per class may increase (Scott, 2003, p. 29). Definitions of intensive courses range from "intensive, compressed, concentrated, or short-term learning" (Serdyukov, 2008, p. 37) to "multi-sensory, brain-compatible teaching and learning methodology" (McKeon, 1995, p. 64). Wlodkowski and Kasworm (2003) believe that intensive learning first of all is "the active learning method of teaching" that allows flexibility and acknowledges students' existing knowledge and experiences (p. 94). However, it is not surprising that some scholars hold quite a negative view of intensive courses. Critics typically point out a lack of time allocated for scaffolding students' learning and reflections on what is being learned (Wlodkowski, 2003). In this respect, the advocates of intensive courses feel pressured to demonstrate the effectiveness of such an educational approach (Swenson, 2003).

The major challenge faced by universities and other institutions offering the intensive mode of course delivery is organizing the learning processes in a way that enables students to take charge of their learning and achieve academic results equivalent to traditional semester courses. While some educators agree that the intensive courses offer more flexible study options, others argue that the intensive learning can be difficult for international students due to the high-paced nature of course delivery, time-constrained projects and a necessity to quickly adapt to a new learning environment. However, a study by Ho and Piven (2015) found that international students prefer the intensive mode of course delivery to a traditional semester due to a timesaving course schedule and more opportunities for feedback and interaction with a lecturer. Moreover, students found themselves more efficient and productive due to having more time for independent leaning.

Even though, intensive courses are gaining popularity among international students, there has been a lack of relevant studies on, and interest in social media as one of the possible solutions that can help international students to overcome challenges associated with the intensive mode of course delivery and to overall enhance their learning experiences.

In closing, being confronted with a need to develop more effective learning environments for international students, tertiary education tends to accept that technology in general and social media may potentially change traditional teaching practices. And the message is clear - there is an obvious gap between educational approaches and the world of international learners. This chapter is intended as a contribution to the research on international students' learning experiences focusing on the intensive courses delivered in a blended format which is through class-based tutorials, Moodle, and closed groups on Facebook. Emerging from the point of view and experiences of international students, the study enriches the conversation on the applicability of social media in the international classroom and presents useful examples for educators who wish to incorporate social media in their courses.

Instrumental Case Study Design and Methodology

In this instrumental study, defined in line with Yin (2003) as "an empirical inquiry that investigates a contemporary phenomenon within its real-life context" (p. 13), Facebook closed groups were set up for two undergraduate courses at Otago Polytechnic Auckland International Campus (OPAIC). OPAIC offers courses for international students only and follows the intensive mode of course delivery that is five terms each year instead of two traditional semesters. OPAIC classes are relatively small - the average class size varies from 12 to 30 students. Each term is comprised of eight weeks of teaching, followed by a two-week break. Such schedule allows students to concentrate on fewer courses at one time (two versus four).

The decision to set up Facebook closed groups for the Event Planning and Entrepreneurship courses was largely motivated by two interrelated factors: the rapid integration of social networks into students' everyday lives and the educational need for international learners to take an active part in determining their study paths and meet the challenges associated with the intensive mode of course delivery. The decision was also encouraged by the current research on social media in education which claims that social media has the potential to help students "not only to improve their teamwork, but also their learning skills" (Bicen & Uzunboylu, 2012, p. 658).

The undergraduate students involved in the study were enrolled in Event Planning and Entrepreneurship courses (level 7). There were 15, 3.5 hour face-to-face tutorials during the term. Both courses were delivered in a blended format including traditional classroom-based teaching, Moodle, and Facebook. In general, Moodle served as a point of departure and course navigation system for students while Facebook was used for real-time conversations and activities. The mode of course delivery and frequency of communication with students on Facebook were the same for both courses. The following Facebook based activities were implemented during both courses delivery:

- **Content Distribution:** A course outline, assessments' instructions, exemplars, guest speakers' presentations, and additional resources such as articles were provided on Facebook under the "Files" menu option throughout the courses.
- **Course Announcements:** Facebook was used as an online information board that kept students informed about guest speakers, field trips, and extra tutorials. Once students subscribed to the class notifications, they automatically received timely updates. Students were also reminded about assessment due dates and notified when the tutor issued the assessment grades.
- **"Before, During and After Class" Activities:** Facebook was used to shift courses towards a flipped classroom. In-class activities were intertwined with Facebook. Students continued working on projects introduced in class or were asked to complete some tasks prior to the next class and post results on Facebook. For example, Entrepreneurship students were asked to post their favorite Kickstarter or Pledge Me project on Facebook and justify their choices. The idea was to check students' understanding of the concept of innovation and use their posts as an opening activity in the next class.
- **Team Projects:** Facebook was used as a collaborative platform for group-based assessments and self-regulated group work. Facebook was adapted for meetings, group discussions, sharing information, exchanging ideas, raising important issues, and keeping teams updated.
- **Reflections on Learning:** Students regularly shared their notes/ images/videos and links relevant to topics covered in class. They also reflected on different class activities such as field trips or events.
- **Questions/Answers Sessions:** Facebook was used to test students' understanding and progress before summative assessments as well as to encourage follow up discussions and peer feedback. Facebook served as a 24/7 support allowing students to ask questions or seek assistance from a lecturer or other students outside the class hours.
- **Summative Assessments:** Facebook was incorporated into project-based summative assessments for both courses. For example, Entrepreneurship students were expected to create a Facebook page for

Figure 1. Course announcements on Facebook: Closed group of the entrepreneurship course, level 6

their business ideas. Event Planning students ran a promo campaign for an event they were organizing.

- **Content Creation:** Facebook was used for student-generated original content that included business pages for start-up businesses (Entrepreneurship course), events (Event Planning course), images, posters, videos, and stories. Content creation was one of the most important elements of the Event Planning course as students were expected to run a social media campaign.

- **Inter-Institutional Collaborations:** Facebook was used to extend course projects beyond Facebook closed groups, focusing on collaboration at the institutional level. For example, Entrepreneurship students' start-up ideas and Event Planning students' event proposals were displayed on the OPAIC Facebook page for voting upon.

A total of 25 Event Planning students and 13 Entrepreneurship students were engaged with the Facebook closed groups during the course delivery. All observation and focus group participants were OPAIC students, mainly

Figure 2. Inter-institutional collaboration on Facebook: Startup idea group project. The Entrepreneurship course, level 6

from China and India, aged between 21 to 33. A total of seven Event Planning students and seven Entrepreneurship students participated in the focus groups on Facebook after their completion of the courses. The study employed a qualitative instrumental case study methodology in which online participant observation of the Event Planning and Entrepreneurship courses had been implemented in triangulation with two asynchronous Facebook focus groups. The choice of methodology was motivated by the exploratory nature of the research question and the characteristics of Facebook, which has a dual function in this study: as the research context and the tool for data collection.

The data was collected in two stages: 1) participant observation on the Event Planning and Entrepreneurship Facebook closed groups between March 2015 and March 2016; 2) two asynchronous Facebook focus groups in April 2016. Evidence from observational data (stage 1) was used as stimuli during the focus groups (stage 2). Such an approach allowed the tutor/researcher to capture international students' activities, reactions and behavior through the participant observation on Facebook, and then to use observational evidence to develop and facilitate a focus group discussion.

The choice of an asynchronous focus group on Facebook was motivated by the idea that "asynchronous communication…allows participants to construct more considered narratives, providing a depth that might be absent in uttered

Table 1. Data collection

Stage	Method of Data Collection	Source of Data
1	Participant observation (Event Planning and Entrepreneurship Facebook closed groups)	International students' narratives/ images/ links/ questions/ comments/ reactions/generated content/ frequency of participation/ group conversations
2	Two asynchronous focus groups on Facebook	International students' reflection on their learning experiences with Facebook closed groups

data" (Stewart & Williams, 2005, p. 413). Mann and Stewart point out that an online focus group "is an efficient and highly-cost-effective mechanism for gathering detailed data, in large quantities" (as cited in Kozinets, 2010, p. 48). It is also important to emphasize that this method is not time restricted. In this respect, an asynchronous online focus group has some obvious advantages over the face-to-face approach. Furthermore, the asynchronous focus group opens up the possibility of increasing the duration of group discussions, which is a big plus if there is a need to cross-test the preliminary research findings.

STUDY RESULTS AND DISCUSSION

The next sections introduce study results related to the following research question: What are the educational values of Facebook for international students enrolled in the intensive courses? The discussion and much of the pedagogical concepts used in the analysis link in one way or another to several guiding questions provided earlier in this chapter. They are as follows:

1. What are international students' views on the intensive courses that incorporate Facebook closed groups as a learning tool?
2. What are international students' views on Facebook as a learning tool in comparison with learning management systems such as Moodle?
3. What are the factors that may impact international students' learning experiences with courses incorporating Facebook?

What is presented further does not claim to be a definitive guide for social media use in the international classroom, and should be seen merely as ideas and suggestions that can help learning designers and teachers to begin incorporating social media into teaching and learning. Based on the guiding research questions above, the discussion breaks down all students' learning experiences into the categories shown in Table 2.

Table 2. Discussion structure

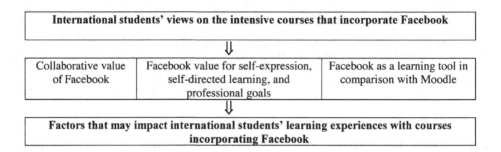

International Students' Views on the Intensive Courses That Incorporate Facebook

I really enjoyed every aspect of the course. I thought it was challenging, meaningful. – Facebook focus group participant (Entrepreneurship course)

The study results indicate that the majority of the research participants welcomed learning opportunities presented on Facebook. Based on the data analysis, international students enrolled in the two intensive business courses recognized a number of Facebook values for learning. This study results have been grouped around two broad categories. First, participants' experiences with Facebook were social and collaborative. These experiences took place in the form of team projects, information search, problem solving, timely feedback, discussions, and shared resources. Second, participants saw a value of Facebook as providing for self-expression, self-directed learning and professional goals. What seems to emerge here is that course-related communications and activities on Facebook boosted international students' confidence and creativity, and enabled them to develop new skills.

Collaborative Value of Facebook

The educational industry's interest in collaborative learning has been motivated by what Smith and MacGregor (1992) call "rich contexts" that "challenge students to practice and develop higher order reasoning and problem-solving skills" (p. 12). According to the authors, "collaborative learning is socially and intellectually involving. It invites students to build closer connections to other students, to their faculty, to their courses, and to their learning" (Smith

32

& MacGregor, 1992, p. 13). In this regard, social media holds out a promise to provide different scenarios for collaboration and triggers "specific learning mechanisms" while students are involved in a "situation in which particular forms of interaction…are expected to occur (Dillenbourg, 2007, p. 4).

Research results show that in general, participants thought that Facebook allows for organizing team projects more effectively. Thus, Facebook greatly contributed to team communications by providing the easiest and fastest way to keep team members updated, share ideas and resources:

Sharing links, new ideas and tips for creating businesses…are useful. It also allows the class to discuss the idea in detail. It [Facebook] allowed communicating with each other outside class and learning collectively. (Entrepreneurship class participant)

Everyone can join the discussion…Facebook is the fastest way to announce what we [team] have done, if there is a problem or suggestions they can reply immediately (Event Planning participant).

This result is consistent with previous research. For example, Rambe (2012) found that Facebook can "complement classroom practices by creating student learning communities for knowledge generation" (p. 309). From students' perspectives, Facebook appeared to be useful for course-related communications outside the class:

It was an amazing team to work with and everyone put in their best…It was different from Moodle and most of all it was very interactive.

Participants also acknowledged Facebook as having the collaborative value that is associated with easy access to resources and information:

Websites like Facebook have people sharing useful links, which can be informational and educational. I access Facebook once or twice daily for 10 to 15 minutes (Entrepreneurship course participant)

What should be emphasized here is that although participants in both Event Planning and Entrepreneurship focus groups pointed out a collaborative value of Facebook, this, however, is not supported by the observational data of the Entrepreneurship course. While the majority of Event Planning participants regularly interacted with each other by commenting, posting, and liking,

Figure 3. Team projects on Facebook: Closed group of the Event Planning course, level 6

Entrepreneurship participants were less active and mainly communicated with the lecturer. Contrary to expectations, peer-to-peer communications are not evident in the observational data. Entrepreneurship participants saw the lecturer as the main point of contact, not their peers. To some extent this was also reflected in some focus group data:

You can create study groups, audio or video lessons, send pictures, graph & facilitate real time communication between a lecturer & students (Entrepreneurship course participant).

It should be noted that some findings on Facebook's collaboration qualities are mixed and differ from previous research which says that Facebook can "encourage discussions" or improve "learning outcomes by facilitating discussions with peers" (Salmon, Ross, Pechenkina, & Chase, 2015, p.6). It seems fair to say that putting students into a collaborative situation on Facebook does not necessarily mean that interactions and collaborative learning automatically occur. Facebook collaborative values perceived by some participants could not be solely related to student-to-student interactions and teamwork. For instance, the lecturer's proximity and engagement on Facebook played the most important role in learning experiences of international students enrolled in the Entrepreneurship course. In contrast, Event Planning participants saw the collaborative value of Facebook for networking, and not only in class settings, but also at the institutional level and far beyond that:

Facebook can be the strongest and best marketing tool for event planning... It [Facebook] helps to make good connection with people. We can use Facebook to generate ideas for event by asking people's opinions before and after the event (Event Planning course participant).

Such results suggest that there is a need to identify what kind of teaching approaches may increase the probability that collaborative learning that involves students with different cultural backgrounds occurs on Facebook. Unfortunately, the study did not produce enough evidence to develop this argument. However, based on Dillenbourg's research (2007) on collaborative learning, it can be suggested that: 1) Facebook based collaboration should be carefully designed with a strong focus on activities and knowledge that "cannot be solved solely with one type of knowledge"; 2) Facebook based collaboration requires specific and clear interaction rules to scaffold effective team communications; 3) Facebook based collaboration needs a regular teacher's input and "minimal pedagogical interventions in order to redirect the group work in a productive direction or to monitor which members are left out of the interaction" (p. 6).

Several other principles for teaching in the international classroom have been put forward by Rovai (2007) who has studied synchronous online discussions that involved culturally diverse students. The author points out that "basic communication rules that may bring success in an intra-cultural context may not be sufficient for a successful inter-cultural interaction" and strongly encourages teachers to help students to get to know each other and learn about each other's cultural background and personal goals (p.84).

Some participants acknowledged the benefits of collaborative learning on Facebook for their personal experiences, cultural adaptation in particular:

I have learned a lot about New Zealand culture through Facebook. For example, I never knew what Anzac day is but then I read an article about Anzac day on Facebook...All these are part of my learning from social media. It is indeed important now for me...it helps me a lot, and in the end I know where I stand with the information I have on a particular subject (Event Planning course participant).

This finding is in line with previous research by Arkiodies et al. (2013), which states that Facebook "may contribute to a more positive international study experience by creating opportunities for overseas students to make

35

digitally mediated points of connection with the host culture" (as cited in Sleeman et al., 2016, p. 401).

Facebook Value for Self-Expression, Self-Directed Learning, and Professional Goals

Based on the observational data from both courses, the study assumes that some participants' learning experiences were often activated by a need for self-expression. It is particularly evident in the Event Planning course where participants regularly posted photos taken during field trips or class activities. Interestingly, those experiences were also linked to participants' professional interests or goals. For example, participants with a background and career prospects in photography took the initiative to capture the class events and share them with their peers on Facebook. The same can be said about course content generated by participants: being provided with a number of collaborative scenarios, participants were able to embrace their professional skills and express themselves through creation of content (e.g. videos, posters) relevant to their professional or personal interests. Surprisingly, some participants continued posting in groups after the course completion. As one Entrepreneurship participant concluded, *"we got a chance to express ourselves"*.

Interestingly, in Bangert's seven principles framework to online teaching, it is stressed that in order to create a unique experience for each learner, there is a need to recognize and acknowledge "a diverse range of academic talents,

Figure 4. Students' feedback on Facebook based activities: Closed group of the Event Planning course, level 6

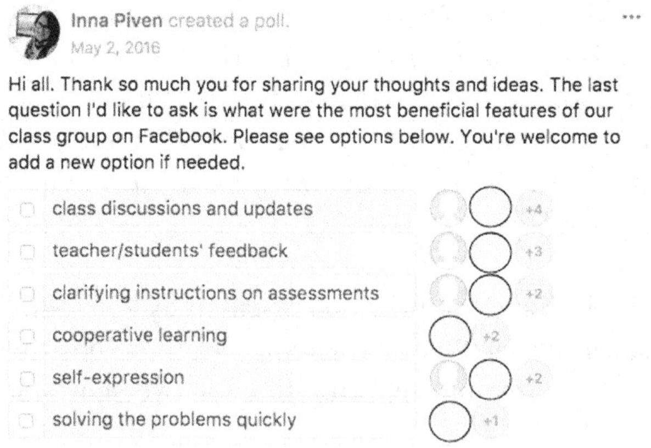

preferences, and experiences" students bring to the educational environment (2006, p. 230). What does it mean in practice? Teachers should create a wide range of activities, which suit international students' learning needs, styles and interests, and offer "multiple opportunities for demonstrating knowledge and skill proficiencies" (Rovai, 2007, p. 84). It is therefore about empowerment and allowing students to make informed decisions and progress towards their personal learning and professional goals.

When designing a course incorporating social media, it is also important to consider international students' future employment opportunities. In comparison with domestic students, international students are faced with a much more difficult time finding a job. The project "The International Student Experience" by Education New Zealand and Study Auckland mentioned earlier, found that "many international students are unaware of what it takes to fit with New Zealand employers" and "the gap between expectations from employers and international students is much greater than we had realized" ("International Student Experience Project", 2017). As said earlier, some research data suggest that students may considerably benefit from social media activities and resources that are associated with their future workplace and industry. More examples related to international students' view on social media as an enabler of employability skills will be presented further when comparing Facebook to Moodle.

Facebook can be used as a learning tool. You gain knowledge from different pages you liked on Facebook for different topics (Event Planning course participant).

In addition, some observational data demonstrate that a number of participants were willing not just to engage with course-related activities on Facebook, but to become an opinion leader by regularly sharing content that they thought might be useful for the class. While the study did not come to a clear conclusion about specific reasons behind such behavior, it can be assumed that through interacting with peers, active posting and sharing on Facebook, participants were able to communicate or shape their self-identity and to some extent satisfy their needs for self-expression. As proposed by Schmidt (2007), "social media facilitate three social cognitive processes: information management, identity management, and relationship management…that result in a change of self-representation…" (as cited in Dabbagh & Kitsantas, 2012, p.4). Although, physiological needs have been well researched in the educational context, the studies on intentional student's self-representation and self-expression in the social media context remain rather silent.

Facebook as a Learning Tool in Comparison With Moodle

Even though there was agreement amongst research participants that Facebook can potentially serve as a learning tool, it was also noted that not all learning activities should be implemented on the social media. The majority of participants believed that Moodle is the best fit for self-directed learning in comparison with Facebook.

Figure 5. Students' reflections on a field trip: Closed group of the Event Planning course, level 6

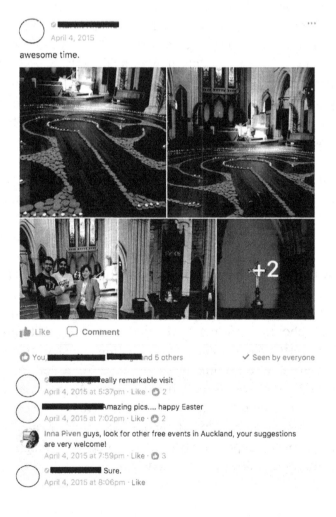

I…prefer Moodle over Facebook…reason being Facebook is more distracting as compared to Moodle. For me Moodle is better if I am learning something new individually…also when I am studying I don't want my notification to popup saying someone liked my picture or something like that…that's what I mean by distracting (Event Planning course participant).

Research results appear to contradict some earlier studies on social media that reported that "Facebook's closed groups are more popular among students than Moodle" (Osepashvili, 2014, p. 378). For example, one of the focus group participants views Facebook "for group announcements and off-class discussion" while Moodle is considered to be "a platform for self-learning". But what participants really gained from Facebook in comparison with Moodle are immediate feedback and the availability of real-time information and communication. By sharing the same platform with different industries, businesses, relevant academic journals and resources, participants were able to direct their learning towards career goals and professional interests.

Facebook is better than any websites because of the response time…I visit Moodle only twice a week (Event Planning course participant).

Facebook can be great for group activities like we did. All our group announcements were over Facebook…None of us used Moodle for group activities, as we are not that active on Moodle (Event Planning course participant).

It is interesting to note that some participants recognized the advantages of Facebook over Moodle for new skills building. Facebook activities incorporated in the course assessments encouraged participants to learn and apply, for example, social media marketing to team projects. Social storytelling and content creation were two key skills students recognized the most. They also found their hands-on experiences with Facebook to be useful for professional development and future employment.

We got to know how to advertise an event through social media, how we can contact a larger audience in just one post. It [Facebook] taught us how to write the right content at the right time (Event Planning course participant).

I use a lot of social networking sites for professional purposes. I follow certain financial consultants and Financial companies like EY, Deloitte, PWC, KPMG, Concentrix, Accenture etc.

It gives me job alerts as I have posted my profile over there so certain employers have contacted me...(Entrepreneurship course participant).

In addition, participants noted that Facebook could be an ideal platform for courses that have more room for creativity, such as marketing, management and entrepreneurship. In general, the study results confirm the previous research on social media that identified the benefits of using social media in creating personal learning environments "that help learners aggregate and share the results of learning achievements, participate in collective knowledge generation, and manage their own meaning making" (Dabbagh & Kitsantas, 2012, p. 2). In this respect, research is needed to analyze the position of self-directed learning in international students' experiences.

Factors That May Impact International Students' Learning Experiences With Courses Incorporating Facebook

The research found it interesting that Event Planning and Entrepreneurship participants responded differently to the same mode of course delivery, types of activities and assessments, and communication style on Facebook. The study reveals that such factors as students' cultural background, class size, type of class activities, other students' engagement, and familiarity with the platform may impact international students' learning experiences with courses delivered on Facebook. For example, one of the research participants noted that the class size and the level of other students' engagement with the course on Facebook might stop some students from being active:

The size of the class, having too many people can lead to less interaction and active participation by all... [...and other students] social media presence. Do they access Facebook regularly or not?

Research results also show that some cultural differences may impact on international students' learning with Facebook. For instance, for Chinese students, it took longer to adapt Facebook for their studies due to a lack of experience, as the network has been blocked in China since 2009. Facebook can be a big "no" for students coming from traditional religious families, for example, for Muslim females. One of the Entrepreneurship class Muslim students could not participate on Facebook because of her family norms and beliefs. To make this student feel included and less isolated, all Facebook based activities were introduced and discussed in class.

It should be noted that students' adjustment to the Facebook classroom did not happen rapidly. At the beginning it was a chaotic experience due to some students' unfamiliarity with the platform and a lack of understanding of reasons why Facebook was incorporated in the course. One participant from the Entrepreneurship course expressed the view that he does not see the learning value of Facebook:

I didn't find any changes in my learning. If you are going to choose other platform such as LinkedIn then it will be more valuable than Facebook (Entrepreneurship course participant).

As mentioned earlier, the intensive course delivery can be challenging for international students as they are expected to learn and apply multiple new concepts within a short space of time. More importantly, the intensive method of teaching may be new to students. That is why it was critical to organize the learning process in a way that enables students to meet challenges presented by the intensive studies. Despite a lack of evidence on the intensive mode of teaching and learning as a contributing factor to participants' experience with Facebook, some observational data show that one of the most common practices the participants were regularly engaged with was asking a lecturer for instructions, clarifications on assessment' requirements, and key dates for release of results.

It was a good idea to convey the message in an easiest way (Entrepreneurship course participant).

It seems that participants recognized the advantages of using Facebook over Moodle for intensive studies, as it offers more opportunities for feedback and interaction with the lecturer.

SOLUTIONS AND RECOMMENDATIONS

Tertiary institutions in the last five years have exhibited a noticeable drift towards innovative forms of teaching in which social media has become a trending topic. Within this context, some directions for social media use in tertiary education with a strong focus on the changing student profile and ongoing technological developments can be identified.

- More focus is needed on self-regulated learning via information/ resources search, networking, and well-designed collaborative projects on social media.
- Implementing social media based cross-disciplinary projects would allow international students to adapt better to a new cultural, social and educational environment.
- It is important to link the assessment strategies to collaborative learning with the use of social media.
- There is a need to recognize and take into consideration students' prior knowledge, their current competences, careers goals and professional interests that can be used as triggers for collaborative learning on social media.

FUTURE RESEARCH DIRECTIONS

Despite a growing awareness of the benefits associated with the courses delivered in a blended format with the use of social media, little coherence exists in education research whether such courses can deliver good results. Hence, empirical evidence focusing on relationships between students' use of social media for learning and their academic performance are much needed. As Irwin, Ball, Desbrow and Leveritt (2012) noted "it is unclear if and how Facebook can enhance student learning outcomes" (p. 1230).

The scarcity of exploratory studies on international students' learning experiences in the context of tertiary education also welcomes further research as well as critical discussion on the educational value of social media. First of all, even though a variety of social media activities has been developed and implemented, students' learning experiences within a relatively new and highly social context of education have not been characterized and conceptualized. As many articles published around students' self-regulated learning and personal learning environments are mainly literature-based, research is needed from the perspectives of actual learners. To understand what self-regulated learning as an educational approach implies in a social media context, future studies should be grounded in concrete learning situations, as learning is always behavior-in-context.

This chapter also encourages dialog on the applicability of social media to the intensive mode of course delivery. Even though the existing research concludes that there is no significant difference between students' performances enrolled in short or full-semester courses (Daniel, 2000), more research is required on international students' experiences of intensive learning with the use of social media.

CONCLUSION

This chapter has presented the results of an instrumental case study undertaken within a four-month period while teaching the Event Planning and Entrepreneurship undergraduate courses at Otago Polytechnic Auckland International Campus, New Zealand. Both courses were delivered in a blended format through class-based teaching, Moodle and Facebook.

To develop a more strategic view on international student learning, the study deployed the instrumental case study methodology and used two methods of data collection (participant observation on Facebook and two asynchronous focus groups) in triangulation. Emerging from the points of view and experiences of international students, the study enriches the conversation on the applicability of social media in the international classroom and produces interesting insights into the educational values of Facebook for collaboration, self-directed learning and professional goals.

One of the most interesting findings is that the majority of research participants tended to prefer Moodle to Facebook for self-directed learning, while Facebook was viewed as a platform for group projects and course announcements. The study also identified some contributing factors that may impact international students' experiences with courses incorporating Facebook including students' cultural background, social media habits, familiarity with the social media platform, as well as class size and level of engagement with course activities.

The study did not find a significant connection between the intensive mode of teaching with the use of Facebook and international students' learning experiences. It seems reasonable to assume that if social media based activities are well-planned and successfully integrated into an institution's learning environment, the mode of course delivery, either intensive or traditional, is not central to students' learning.

The importance of this study can be appreciated in the context of ongoing discussions about new models of delivering education in response to changes in technology and the continuing internationalization of tertiary education.

REFERENCES

Alfarhoud, Y. T., Alahmad, B., Alqahtani, L., & Alhassan, A. (2016). The experience of international students using social media during classes. *International Journal of Education*, *8*(2), 32–47. doi:10.5296/ije.v8i2.9224

Baird, D. E., & Fisher, M. (2005-2006). Neomillennial user experience design strategies: Utilizing social networking media to support "always on" learning styles. *Journal of Educational Technology Systems*, *34*(1), 5–32. doi:10.2190/6WMW-47L0-M81Q-12G1

Bangert, A. W. (2006). The development of an instrument for assessing online teaching effectiveness. *Journal of Educational Computing Research*, *35*(3), 227–244. doi:10.2190/B3XP-5K61-7Q07-U443

Beer, D., & Burrows, R. (2010). Consumption, prosumption and participatory web cultures. *Journal of Consumer Culture*, *10*(3), 3–12. doi:10.1177/1469540509354009

Bicen, H., & Uzunboylu, H. (2013). The use of social networking sites in education: A case study of Facebook. *Journal of Universal Computer Science*, *19*(5), 658–671.

Dabbagh, N., & Kitsantas, A. (2011). Personal learning environments, social media, and self-regulated learning: A natural formula for connecting formal and informal learning. *Internet and Higher Education, 15*(1), 3–8. doi:10.1016/j.iheduc.2011.06.002

Davies, W. M. (2006). Intensive teaching formats: A review. *Issues in Educational Research, 16*(1), 1–20.

Dillenbourg, P. (1999). What do you mean by collaborative learning? In P. Dillenbourg (Ed.), *Collaborative learning: Cognitive and computational approaches* (pp. 1–19). Oxford, UK: Elsevier.

Fischer, E., & Reuber, A. R. (2011). Social interaction via new social media: (How) can interactions on Twitter affect thinking and behavior? *Journal of Business Venturing, 26*(1), 1–18. doi:10.1016/j.jbusvent.2010.09.002

Gerritsen, J. (2017). *Foreign student numbers jump.* Retrieved from http://www.radionz.co.nz/news/national/329800/foreign-student-numbers-jump

Gray, K., Lucas, A., & Kennedy, G. (2010). Medical students' use of Facebook to support learning: Insights from four case studies. *Medical Teacher, 32*(12), 971–976. doi:10.3109/0142159X.2010.497826 PMID:21090950

Guess, A. (2008). *Facebook, meet Blackboard.* Retrieved from https://www.insidehighered.com/news/2008/05/14/sync

Heinonen, K. (2011). Consumer activity in social media: Managerial approaches to consumers' social media behavior. *Journal of Consumer Behaviour, 10*(6), 356–364. doi:10.1002/cb.376

Heinrichs, J. H., Lim, J.-S., & Lim, K.-S. (2011). Influence of social networking site and user access method on social media evaluation. *Journal of Consumer Behaviour, 10*(6), 347–355. doi:10.1002/cb.377

Ho, H. W. L., & Piven, I. (2015, May). *Perceptions of international students on intensive learning at a tertiary institution in New Zealand.* Paper presented at the Sixth Annual Scholarship of Teaching and Learning Academy Conference at the University of Findlay.

Hoffman, D. L., & Novak, T. P. (2012, January 17). *Why do people use social media? Empirical findings and a new theoretical framework for social media goal pursuit.* Retrieved from Social Science Research Network http://papers.ssrn.com/sol3/papers.cfm?abstract_id=1989586

Hootsuite. (2017). *The social revolution: Redefining the student experience in Australian higher education institutions.* Retrieved from https://hootsuite. com/resources/the-social-revolution-australia-higher-education#

International Student Experience Project. (2017). *ATEED & Education New Zealand.* Retrieved from https://intellilab.enz.govt.nz/document/270-2017-international-student-experience-project

International students enrolled in tertiary education. (2017). Retrieved from https://www.educationcounts.govt.nz/statistics/indicators/main/student-engagement-participation/international_students_enrolled_in_formal_tertiary_education

Irwin, C., Ball, L., Desbrow, B., & Leveritt, M. (2012). Students' perceptions of using Facebook as an interactive learning resource at university. *Australasian Journal of Educational Technology, 28*(7), 1221–1232. doi:10.14742/ajet.798

Jih-Hsuan, L., Kim, W. P., Kim, M., Kim, S. Y., & LaRose, R. (2012). Social networking and adjustments among international students. *New Media & Society, 14*(3), 421–440. doi:10.1177/1461444811418627

Journey to transformational student experience. (2017). Retrieved from https://enz.govt.nz/news-and-research/ed-news/journey-to-transformational-student-experience-2/

Kaplan, A. M., & Haenlein, M. (2010). Users of the world, unite! The challenges and opportunities of Social Media. *Business Horizons, 53*(1), 59–68. doi:10.1016/j.bushor.2009.09.003

Kozinets, R. V. (2010). *Netnography: Doing ethnographic research online.* Los Angeles, CA: Sage.

McKeon, K. J. (1995). What is this thing called accelerated learning? *Training & Development, 49*(6), 64–66.

New Zealand Productivity Commission Report. (2017). *New models of tertiary education: Final Report.* Retrieved from https://www.productivity.govt. nz/sites/default/files/New%20models%20of%20tertiary%20education%20 FINAL_3.pdf

Osepashvili, D. (2014). The using of social media platform in modern journalism education. In *Proceedings of the European Conference on Social Media* (pp. 378-387). Brighton, UK: University of Brighton.

Rahman, N. (2014). The usage and online behavior of social networking sites among international students in New Zealand. *The Journal of Social Media in Society, 3*(2), 65–81.

Rambe, P. (2012). Critical discourse analysis of collaborative engagement in Facebook postings. *Australasian Journal of Educational Technology, 28*(2), 295–314. doi:10.14742/ajet.875

Roblyer, M. D., McDaniel, M., Webb, M., Herman, J., & Witty, J. V. (2010). Findings on Facebook in higher education: A comparison of college faculty and student uses and perceptions of social networking sites. *Internet and Higher Education, 13*(3), 134–140. doi:10.1016/j.iheduc.2010.03.002

Rovai, A. P. (2007). Facilitating online discussions effectively. *The Internet and Higher Education, 10*(1), 77–88. doi:10.1016/j.iheduc.2006.10.001

Ryan, S., Magro, M., & Sharp, J. (2011). Exploring educational and cultural adaptation through social networking sites. *Journal of Information Technology Education: Innovations in Practice, 10*, 1–16.

Salmon, G., Ross, B., Pechenkina, E., & Chase, A. (2015). The space for social media in structured online learning. *Research in Learning Technology, 23*(1), 28507. doi:10.3402/rlt.v23.28507

Scott, P. A. (2003). Attributes of high-quality intensive courses. *New Directions for Adult and Continuing Education, 97*(97), 29–38. doi:10.1002/ace.86

Seo, H., Harn, R., Ebrahim, H., & Aldana, J. (2016). International students' social media use and social adjustment. *First Monday, 21*(11), 11–17. doi:10.5210/fm.v21i11.6880

Serdyukov, P. (2008). Accelerated learning: What is it? *Journal of Research in Innovative Teaching, 1*(1), 35–59.

Sherry, M., Thomas, P., & Chui, W. H. (2010). International students: A vulnerable students population. *Higher Education, 60*(1), 33–46. doi:10.100710734-009-9284-z

Sleeman, J., Lang, C., & Lemon, N. (2016). Social media challenges and affordances for international students: Bridges, boundaries, and hybrid spaces. *Journal of Studies in International Education, 20*(5), 391–415. doi:10.1177/1028315316662975

Smith, B. L., & MacGregor, J. T. (1992). What is collaborative learning? In A. S. Goodsell (Ed.), *Collaborative learning: A sourcebook for higher education* (pp. 10–30). University Park, PA: National Center on Postsecondary Teaching, Learning, and Assessment.

Stewart, K., & Williams, M. (2005). Researching online populations: The use of online focus groups for social research. *Qualitative Research, 5*(4), 395–416. doi:10.1177/1468794105056916

Swenson, G. (2003). Accelerated and traditional formats: Using learning as a criterion for quality. *New Directions for Adult and Continuing Education, 97*(97), 83–93. doi:10.1002/ace.91

Toffler, A. (1980). *The third wave* (1st ed.). New York: Bantam Books.

Welikala, T. (2015). *Universities don't understand how international students learn*. Retrieved from https://www.theguardian.com/higher-education-network/2015/jul/03/universities-dont-understand-how-international-students-learn

Wlodkowski, R. J. (2003). Accelerated learning for adults. *New Directions for Adult and Continuing Education, 97*, 5–15. doi:10.1002/ace.84

Wlodkowski, R. J., & Kasworm, C. E. (2003). Accelerated learning: Future roles and influences. *New Directions for Adult and Continuing Education, 97*(97), 93–97. doi:10.1002/ace.92

Wu, H. P., Garza, E., & Guzman, N. (2015). International student's challenge and adjustment to college. *Education Research International, 2015*, 1–9. doi:10.1155/2015/202753

Yin, R. K. (2003). *Case study research: Design and methods* (3rd ed.). Thousand Oaks, CA: Sage.

Zhao, X. (2016). *Social media and the international student experience*. International Education Association of Australia. Retrieved from https://www.ieaa.org.au/documents/item

KEY TERMS AND DEFINITIONS

Blended Learning: The process of gaining and applying knowledge, skills, and experiences through the combination of traditional classroom based activities and digital media tools.

Collaborative Learning: An educational approach that focuses on social contexts of learning. This approach allows students to undertake complex projects and tasks working in teams.

Facebook Closed Group: A type of private group in which all group members have to be approved an administrator prior to joining the group, and only group members can see posted content.

Flipped Classroom: A teaching method where students' learning of a new subject begins prior to in-class tutorials via reading or implementing some activities, and class time is used to develop a deeper understanding of the subject through research, analysis and application of knowledge.

Intensive Mode of Course Delivery: A course delivery option that offers a different timetabling scheduling that allows learners to complete the course in a shorter time frame.

Inter-Institutional Collaborations: A type of collaborative learning that involves communication and networking at the institutional level and engages staff and students from all departments. The purpose of such collaboration is to enhance students' learning through designing, implementing and managing higher-level team projects and showcasing their skills.

International Students: Non-New Zealand students studying at a university or other tertiary education institutions.

Learning Experiences: The process of gaining knowledge and skills through systematic study, practice, and reflections.

Learning Management Systems: Web-based applications used to plan, create, deliver, and document course content and activities.

Moodle: A learning management system that allows organizing and managing course contents, resources, activities, and administrative matters.

Online Learning Environments: Ubiquitous learning settings created through digital devices and social media that enable learning at any time, and provide interactive forms of course activities, resources, and delivery of content.

Project-Based Assessments: A type of assessment based on a project or series of projects that require students to apply diverse knowledge, skills, and strategies to real-world scenarios, problems, or tasks for an extended period of time.

Self-Regulated/Self-Directed or Independent Learning: A process in which students take control of their own learning by understanding their learning needs and goals, identifying appropriate resources and tools, and ways of learning.

Social Media as a Learning Tool: The use of social media in course design and delivery, including content areas, resources, learning activities, and assessments.

Student-Centered Course Design: An approach to course design in which students' learning needs and goals, current knowledge, and skills are central to course content, learning outcomes, resources, activities, and assessments.

Summative Assessments: A type of assessment that evaluates students' academic achievements against learning outcomes related to knowledge and skill acquisition outlined in the course description. Summative assessments are typically scheduled at the end of semester, study block, or unit, and are formally graded and carry weighting toward a student's final grade.

Chapter 3

Navigating the Social Media Space for Māori and Indigenous Communities

Maryann Lee
Unitec Institute of Technology, New Zealand

ABSTRACT

This chapter explores how Māori and Indigenous communities are engaging in social media in ways that reflect their cultural aspirations and Indigenous ways of being. Social media provides opportunities for Indigenous people to represent an Indigenous worldview that encompasses cultural, political, and social preferences. Highlighted also in this chapter are the risks inherent within the use of social media for Māori and Indigenous communities: in ways in which the misrepresentation, commodification, and exploitation of Indigenous culture and traditions are amplified through the use of social media that support colonial ideologies and the ongoing practice of colonization.

INTRODUCTION

This chapter explores how Māori and Indigenous groups are engaging in social media in ways that reflect our cultural aspirations and Indigenous ways of being. I argue that social media provides opportunities to create new spaces to reflect an Indigenous worldview, which encompasses cultural, political and social preferences. This includes advancing an agenda of self-determination that challenges colonial ideologies and western constructs of

DOI: 10.4018/978-1-5225-5826-2.ch003

colonization (Pihama, 2001). I also highlight the risks inherent within the use of social media for Māori and Indigenous communities; and how social media can be used to perpetuate the ongoing practice of colonization, which systematically sets out to maintain the power and control of the dominant society (Iseke-Barne, 2002).

Due to the lack of literature published on social media and Indigenous people within tertiary education (Huijser & Bronnimann, 2014), this chapter provides a Kaupapa Māori framework for better understanding Māori and Indigenous engagement in social media in general. Establishing this broader context serves to introduce some of the motivations, considerations and aspirations of Māori and Indigenous people in the use of social media. In this regard, this chapter prefaces a case-study in chapter four, about the use of Facebook to support Māori doctoral scholars and academics within the New Zealand tertiary environment. For Māori, educational aspirations are not limited to educational contexts and individual success; they have much wider implications that impact on whānau (family), hapū (sub-tribe) and iwi (tribe). Therefore, understanding the context of how Māori and Indigenous groups engage in social media as a decolonizing process for the transformation of Indigenous communities is critical and relevant for all educators. This chapter begins with an introduction to a Kaupapa Māori approach, followed by a discussion on ways in which Māori and Indigenous people are using social media to support our cultural aspirations, drawing on three Kaupapa Māori principles. The final section highlights the risks associated with social media for Indigenous communities in relation to the exploitation and commodification of indigenous culture; the racial discrimination against, and misrepresentation of, Indigenous people; and the disruption of Indigenous ways of being.

A KAUPAPA MĀORI APPROACH

This analysis is underpinned by a Kaupapa Māori methodological approach that draws from a Māori knowledge base and lived experiences. Kaupapa Māori promotes the validity of Māori language, knowledge and culture (Pihama, 2001). Kaupapa Māori supports Māori academics to carry out research in ways that embrace the values and principles of our whānau, hapū and iwi (L. Smith, 2003). Linda Smith (2003) asserts that Kaupapa Māori research comes from a local Indigenous theoretical position; a philosophy that encompasses a Māori worldview including spiritual, cultural and political dimensions.

The Kaupapa Māori methodological approach enables Māori academics to participate in research that draws from ontological worldviews, and embraces Māori tikanga and values (L. Smith, 2003).

Kaupapa Māori also provides a theoretical and political tool as a basis for Indigenous researchers to work as change agents and to engage in research that is transformative for Indigenous people (G. Smith, 2003). Linda Smith (2003) believes that recognizing the injustices of colonization and thinking about ways that we can resist and challenge colonial ideologies is the first step to decolonization. She argues that while there is often an illusion that colonization is no longer practiced, there are still "new forms of colonization" which have been reformed in more subtle ways and, "many of these formations are insidious, and many of them have yet to be fully explored" (L. Smith, 2003, p. 215). Social media can be considered as one of these forms that often appear neutral, a-cultural and decolonized.

Graham Smith's (2003) discussion on Kaupapa Māori emphasizes the need to uncover injustices experienced by underprivileged groups, and recognizes the powerlessness that individuals may feel about their own destinies. He points out that Māori are struggling from the injustices of the past, whether they are aware of this or not. In Graham Smith's view, Māori are located within three intervention areas: conscientization, a 'freeing' of the Indigenous mind from the dominant hegemony; resistance, or going outside the constraints of the dominant system; transformative action, or engaging in a radical pedagogy and becoming change agents (G. Smith, 2003, p. 13). These areas are not independent of each other, nor do they fall in a linear order. Instead, they represent a cyclic approach whereby all Māori can be plotted somewhere within the cycle of Kaupapa Māori praxis. This is an important critique to assist in better understanding Māori engagement in social media with a Kaupapa Māori agenda.

KAUPAPA MĀORI CONSIDERATIONS FOR SOCIAL MEDIA

Graham Smith (2003) has identified six principles as a way of understanding Kaupapa Māori theory. These principles are: Tino rangatiratanga, self determination principle; Taonga tuku iho, cultural aspirations principle; Ako, Māori, culturally preferred pedagogy principle; Kia piki ake i ng ā raruraru o te kainga, the mediation of socio-economic factors; Whānau, extended family structure principle; Kaupapa, collective philosophy principle (G. Smith, 2003). While I have drawn on three principles in this chapter to help frame a way of thinking about Māori engagement in the social media space, the Kaupapa Māori principles reflect the lived experiences as Māori. Therefore, the principles are not seen in isolation, and will often overlap within the various themes discussed.

While this chapter often refers to the use of social media by Indigenous communities in a more general way, it is important to acknowledge that these communities are hugely diverse in geographical locations, politics and cultural traditions. For example, the use of social media amongst Amazonian Indigenous people varies considerably between the urban population and the rainforest inhabitants (Virtanen, 2015). In addition, social media applications provide different tools that are used widely for a range of purposes by Indigenous groups. This section attempts to highlight some examples of the ways in which Indigenous communities are using social media, including; political activism, cultural revitalization; and building stronger relationships and connections amongst Indigenous communities.

Tino Rangatiratanga: Self-Determination Principle

'Tino rangatiratanga' is a central principle of Kaupapa Māori theory. Self-determination, autonomy and sovereignty are ways to express tino rangatiratanga, whereby Māori can make decisions and choices both individually and collectively (Pihama, 2001). Fundamental to tino rangatiratanga is the acknowledgement of Māori epistemologies that promote Māori worldviews, knowledge, language and culture as authoritative and valid. Cultural identity and aspirations of Māori can only be achieved through a Māori worldview that is defined by and for Māori. Additionally, tino rangatiratanga is often viewed as a direct protest to the Crown, and seeks to legitimize the rights of whānau, hapū and iwi. It is intrinsically linked to Te Tiriti o Waitangi, that guarantees the right for Māori sovereignty as tangata whenua (people of the land) and is seen as a binding document with the Crown (Pihama, 2001).

The notion of tino rangatiratanga aligns with an Indigenous agenda of self-determination, and provides a way of thinking about how social media can be used as a political space in pursuit of sovereignty (Waitoa, Scheyvens, & Warren, 2015). For instance, in an examination of the use of social media by the Mana Party in the 2011 New Zealand elections, Waitoa (2013) found that social media gave the Mana party greater ownership and control of their content to key audiences. This aligned with the aim of the Mana Party as articulated by Annette Sykes, to "increase political participation through the ability to acquire greater political knowledge, increase political interest, improve political self-efficacy and highlight different perspectives and political opinion on what media portrays to us" (Waitoa, 2013, p. 73). Waitoa points out that social media sites enable the Mana party to represent themselves and their perspectives directly to their key constituents - Māori communities.

Social media also enables individuals, who may not have previously seen themselves as politically active, to become strong Indigenous advocates through the re-posting of protests, sharing of images, narratives and commentaries (Duarte, 2017). In fact, political activism can take place through the 'mundane' use of social media by Indigenous people's 'self-writing' about everyday life (Petray, 2013). It can be a powerful tool to normalize Indigenous views that challenge mainstream stereotypes, allowing opportunities to create a collective online identity to support Indigenous movements (Petray, 2013).

Dr. Adrienne Keene, from the Cherokee Nation, is a strong example of how an individual blogger can contribute and connect to the much larger online community. As a Native student in an elite institution, Adrienne Keene's feelings of isolation and separation from her classmates were the catalyst for her seeking connections online. Her blog, entitled 'Native Appropriations,' examines representations of Indigenous people, focusing on issues of cultural appropriation and stereotyping. "Writing the blog gave me voice. In my semi-anonymous space on the Internet, I was free to question, be angry, and fight back-things I struggled to do in 'real life'. I watched my notoriety and influence grow online, while in my day-to-day I was still a silent girl in the back of the classroom" (Keene, 2013). Adrienne Keene now has over 100,000 followers on her Native Appropriations Facebook page, and continues to blog, as well as use Twitter and Instagram to advocate and politicize Indigenous issues.

Indigenous movements such as the EZLN, Idle No More, and the Rio Yaqui water rights, highlighted in Duarte's (2017) research, use strong social media tactics to destabilize dominant governments and neoliberal political economies. The ability to engage in social network sites, in ways that are far less regulated than other political forums, enables a range of tactics to be employed by activists. Additionally, social media offers opportunities for marginalized groups within Indigenous communities to speak out and challenge oppressive politics (Parkhurst, 2017). For example, the 'Archiving the Aboriginal Rainbow blog project' that represents the Aboriginal and Torres Strait Islander LGBTIQ peoples to assert their political positions, draw attention to their oppression and challenge violence faced by their community

(Farrell, 2017). Belton (2010) supports this view, and highlights how the digital spaces enable more opportunity to articulate for political expression;

Cyberspace thus allows those who are marginalized to speak more easily in their own voices without having to go through approved representatives or channels. As a result, Indigenous peoples may demand boycotts and strikes, alert the world of human rights violations, and share political tactics and ancestral stories without having to be a present, identified body. (Belton, 2010, p. 197)

There are strong examples in New Zealand where social media networks are being used to mobilize Indigenous movements, as well as build momentum for these projects with non-Indigenous allies. The 'SOUL - Save Our Unique Landscape' Campaign exemplifies a social media articulation of tino rangatiratanga at Ōtuataua in Mangere, Auckland. Led by young Māori women, such as Pania Newton, a number of protests have taken place against the proposal for the development of 480 homes in Ihumatao on land that has historical and sacred significance to the local tribal groups and community. The use of social media platforms, including Facebook, YouTube and Twitter, has helped to galvanize support at both a local and international scale (http://www.soulstopsha.org/). Additionally, a virtual occupation of the land, with over 4000 people symbolically residing on the site to protest against the development, has drawn wide attention. Strong use of social media tactics has provided a small local protest with a much larger support base throughout New Zealand and beyond. It has also inspired other Indigenous communities experiencing similar corporate land battles.

Taonga Tuku Iho: Cultural Aspirations Principal

Taonga tuku iho is closely linked to tino rangatiratanga, and is the principle, acknowledging Māori knowledge and traditions, that continues to sustain and support whānau, hapū and iwi to live as Māori. Taonga tuku iho validates Māori ways of being and creates a space for Māori to 'be Māori', whereby cultural aspirations and identity are legitimized (G. Smith, 2003). In the face of colonization, Māori have struggled to maintain the Māori language, cultural practices and protocols. In particular, the systematic denial of the Māori language through the advancement of colonial ways has impacted negatively on Māori communities (Pihama & Cameron, 2012). The principle of taonga tuku iho is illustrated through the use of social media in a range of ways to revive and maintain Indigenous traditional culture and language, and create digital spaces that reflect cultural aspirations.

One advantage of social media is the ease with which dynamic content can be created and shared across social networks. The recording and production of spoken language, as well as music, arts and dance, enables Indigenous communities to revitalize and reinvigorate languages and cultural practices struggling to be sustained in contemporary contexts (Alexander, 2010). Social media provides an opportunity to express and represent Indigenous worldviews in ways that are responsive to Indigenous ways of being. For example, digital storytelling enables Indigenous people to control their images and narratives through their own self-representations and, in doing so, challenge the stereotypical representation by the dominant society (Iseke & Moore, 2011). Iseke and Moore (2011) state, "Collecting community stories through digital means ensures that communities honor their oral traditions and resist the dominance of texts that are prevalent in the dominant society" (p. 35). Publishing on the web can also challenge the authority of Western representations in media and texts, and disrupt the 'elite' forms of traditional publishing (Nakata, 2002). Nakata states;

The online environment has reconstituted the balance between visual, oral, and textual modes of presenting information in a way that supports cultural perspectives. Further, the Web supports publishing in ways that disrupt established 'elite' forms of publication and which 'authorize' previously excluded groups from publishing. (Nakata, 2002, p. 28)

Also highlighted in the literature are ways in which social media offers Indigenous people the ability to reflect their own identities. While social media can be a space to explore identity, Carlson (2013) suggests that those who identify themselves as Indigenous offline will tend to be no different in how they identify themselves online. Therefore, by simply engaging in social media networks, Indigenous peoples project their indigeneity and reflect their cultural interests, preferences, beliefs and practices (Carlson, 2013; Lumby, 2010). Expressing one's indigeneity on social media, Lumby (2010) argues, is not just a matter of 'being' Indigenous, but more a matter of 'doing' indigeneity. For example, in Facebook, creating member profiles, accepting 'friends', belonging to groups, liking, sharing and commenting of content etc. all directly contribute to developing a representation of one's self.

The revitalization and preservation of Indigenous languages is another cultural aspiration that supports the taonga tuku iho principle. Māori have been innovative in their approach to promoting and normalizing Māori language in its everyday use, and many are using social media as a way to support this. In 2014 Pita Paraone, the chief executive for The Māori Language Commission, called for social media to be 'swamped' with the Māori language. He states, "Social media is a new frontier for Māori language use. Māori language speakers encourage others when they use te reo Māori as their default language for tweeting and messaging" (Rotorua Daily Post, 2004). Research undertaken by Keegan, Mato and Ruru (2015) indicate this to be occurring amongst Māori in the use of Twitter. They found a vibrant community of minority language tweeters who were able to connect with each other despite their geographical distance. Keegan, Mato and Ruru (2015) identified 90,000 tweets in Te Reo Māori (Māori language), and while many were both commercial and religious tweets, there were a number of individuals using twitter to converse in Te Reo.

As discussed in chapters two and five of this book, the use of social media for teaching and learning within tertiary environments is becoming more prevalent, as teachers explore ways to engage students that encompass digital learning environments. The notion of ako as a cultural pedagogical framework is closely aligned to taonga tuku iho and is also one of Graham Smith's (1991) Kaupapa Māori principles. For Māori, ako provides a more holistic and non-linear approach to teaching and learning. Ako can also be used to define the cultural aspirations for Māori education within our society. Lee (2008) asserts that ako does not just refer to teaching and learning processes but that "ako refers to a Māori educational framework that was integral in the protection, sustenance and transmission of knowledge, shaped by what was collectively deemed necessary and important" (p. 108).

Therefore, when exploring the use of social media and online learning communities with Māori and Indigenous students, there are a number of factors to consider that contribute towards a more culturally responsive teaching and learning framework (Dashper, 2017; Tiakiwai & Tiakiwai, 2008). For example, the ITPNZ report (2004) highlights the views of Māori educators and e-learning specialists during a two-day hui which looked at the concept of ako and how it may be applied to e-learning. It was suggested that, rather than use the term e-'learning', they preferred the term 'e-ako', as it represented the holistic and aspirational nature for Māori that includes both 'teaching *and* learning'. One participant asserts, "Ako is a whole lot of interlinked concepts such as whānau. It does not stand alone ... E-ako cannot be reduced to models or rules or too strict a definition" (ITPNZ, 2014, p. 31). Such views highlight how the use of social media for teaching and learning cannot be viewed in isolation, but must incorporate the principle of taonga tuku iho that acknowledge the cultural aspirations and identity of the learner. The complexities involved in engaging in a Kaupapa Māori community of learners are highlighted and explored in the following chapter.

Huijser and Bronnimann (2014) discuss social media for Indigenous learning by drawing on Yunkaporta's 2009 'eight-way framework of Aboriginal Pedagogy'. The framework includes the following concepts: story sharing; community links; deconstruct/ reconstruct; non-linear; land links; symbols & images; non-verbal; and learning maps. Huijser and Bronnimann (2014) highlight a range of social media tools that can support each of the eight concepts and in turn provide opportunities to align with a more Indigenous learning context. They assert;

... social media allow us to start the learning process from where Indigenous students are at, and allow us to draw on existing knowledge, rather than simply imposing a knowledge set on them, because we (as in western educators) have decided that is what they should know. (Huijser & Bronnimann, 2014, p. 102)

For Indigenous students, there are benefits for engaging in social media in order to enable a more learner-centered and holistic pedagogy that aligns more strongly to an Indigenous educational framework.

Whānau: Extended Family Structure Principle

While whānau is defined as a family group or extended family which is brought together through whakapapa (genealogy), whānau can also be used metaphorically to refer to a group of people who are working to a common end. Whānau *values*, particularly if kinship connections are absent, are what governs relationships with each other and connects the group (Metge,19 95). Pihama (2001) argues that colonization has actively targeted whānau structures and presented an individualist ideological view of a 'nuclear family'. Therefore, the terms 'whānau' and 'family' are not the same and Kaupapa Māori initiatives seek to affirm the roles and responsibilities of a collective whānau group. Being part of a whānau means there is a strong commitment to provide support to other whanau members, particularly for those who cannot fend for themselves. Inherent in a whānau structure are certain rights, responsibilities and obligations that are implicit within whānau relationships (Pihama, 2001).

Social media can support the notion of whānau in ways that foster connection, sharing, and co-creating amongst online communities (Bell, Budka, & Fiser, 2007; Molyneaux et al., 2014). For Indigenous people, particularly those who have become dislocated from their tribal land and communities, social media offers a way to connect back to their homelands. Molyneaux's et al. (2014) research surveyed 633 people from geographically remote First Nation communities, in the Sioux Look Out region of north western Ontario. Amongst their findings, participants frequently used social network sites, with 72.8% reporting daily. Their research highlighted a positive correlation between how often people communicated to each other on social media outside their communities, and the frequency of traveling outside their communities. Such findings support a link between online communication and face-to-face contact (Molyneaux et al., 2014). Molyneaux et al's (2014) research also found that their participants "use the Internet or social media to celebrate and practice their culture. More than half post photographs and stories and listen to music and look at art created by Aboriginal people on SNSs" (p. 285). Through the sharing of cultural resources and exchanging of information through social media, Indigenous people are developing stronger connections amongst each other and building resilience within their communities. (Molyneaux et al., 2014).

The principle of whānau is a significant factor for Māori engagement within social media. O'Carroll (2013) examines how rangatahi (youth) use social network sites to facilitate whānau connections and communication. Her research found that many of her participants actively sought to use social network sites to engage with whānau and to increase their whānau ties and relationships. O'Carroll (2013) states, "Whanaungatanga practice in virtual spaces was underpinned with the same values and principles as those practiced in physical spaces. Enabling whānau members to connect to each other helped them to nurture their familial relationships" (p. 278). O'Carroll's research indicated that social media enabled them to maintain values of whanaungatanga, identity and tikanga, which they already experienced in a physical way, through their online engagement as well.

Additionally, the use of social media sites has enabled iwi, hapū and whānau to re-connect, communicate with and support their whānau. This is reflected in many of the Māori tribal Facebook groups that are active today. One example, The Waikato Tainui Facebook page launched in 2013, is using social media to reach out to its 65,000 descendants in Aotearoa and abroad. On their Facebook they state, "As a tribal entity we aim to empower our people by providing a range of programmes and opportunities including grants and scholarships, education and health programmes, employment and training, cultural initiatives and marae development assistance" (https://www.facebook.com/Waikato.Te.Iwi/).

CHALLENGES

While the previous section outlines some of the ways in which Māori and Indigenous are engaging in digital spaces aligned to Kaupapa Māori principles, this section draws attention to the implications and complexities that are implicit within online engagement. It also looks at some of the key challenges that social media presents to Māori and Indigenous communities. This section seeks to challenge mainstream ideologies prevalent in the Western dominant society reflected in social media sites; in particular, the exploitation and misrepresentation of Indigenous culture and traditions.

Commodification and Misrepresentation

Indigenous groups must now contend with the global digitalization of their cultural possessions being robbed and distributed for commercial gain (Iseke-Barnes & Danard, 2007). Offering even greater access to audiences as well as unrestricted commercial opportunities, the internet is participating in the commodification of Indigenous culture and knowledge. Iseke-Barnes and Danard, (2007) discuss how Indigenous symbols and representations lose all cultural significance once they become commodities. For example, the dreamcatcher, which is a spiritual symbol from the Ojibwe people, is now being sold and purchased on hundreds of thousands of websites around the world without any historical or cultural context. "The cultural significance of the dreamcatcher is erased. It simply becomes a commodity" (Iseke-Barnes & Danard, 2007, p. 29).

In addition, the misappropriation and exploitation of tribal stories via social media poses adverse risk for Indigenous people. For Māori, tribal pūrākau (stories) has been a way for Māori to retain ancestral knowledge and to portray the lives of their tupuna (ancestors). Māori can reclaim pūrākau for purposeful and pedagogical narrative, in a way that advances Māori educational aspirations and offers a counter-story to the dominant discourse (Lee, 2008). However, Lee (2008) warns of the misappropriation of pūrākau through the translation and homogenizing of myths and legends and where such stories, collated through a colonizer's perspective, portray misrepresentations of Māori.

A strong example of traditional story-telling being portrayed through a colonizer's perspective is the Walt Disney movie *Moana* that was marketed widely through social media channels in 2016. The movie presented stereotypical characters of Pacifika people, in particular Maui, who is depicted as an obese Polynesian. These representations were amplified through the sharing, liking and commenting across social networks globally. Associate Professor Leonie Pihama used social media to 'write back' and protest against the misappropriation of the movie. She asserts, "You see Moana is not our story. It is not our representation of ourselves. It does not reflect any particular nation. It is a generalised, universalised, pan-nation, colonised, exploitation that is based on what... a bunch of white men reading Gaugin" (Pihama, 2016a). Within a year of the movie coming out, advertisements were circulating on social media networks for actors who could speak the Māori language. Pihama posts again;

If this film is translated directly into te reo Māori it will contribute to the colonising beliefs about being Indigenous and will be of more danger to the ways our tamariki understand being Māori than anything else. Translations of colonial beliefs reproduce colonial beliefs. The whole script must be decolonized and rewritten before being recreated in te reo Māori. (Pihama, 2016b).

Despite Pihama's Facebook protests, the script was translated into Māori and the movie released during Māori language week in 2017. An opportunity to re-tell a traditional pūrākau in a way that reflected and honored the rich cultural beliefs and value of the Pacific and Māori people has been lost to a Walt
Disney commercial venture, that was reported to have earned over $600 million at the worldwide box office (Mendelson, 2017).

Racial Discrimination

Racial discrimination and hatred exists within the Internet in many forms. While the anonymity of cyberspace enables people to engage in an indiscriminate way, without having to identify their country or culture, it can also fuel racist attitudes and actions towards ethnic groups that are perceived as a threat.

Social media platforms are not excluded from the harboring of racial attitudes and racial attacks on Indigenous peoples (Carlson, Jones, Harris, Quezada, & Frazer, 2017).

The anonymous nature of the Internet can also enable racial attacks through stolen identities and false portrayal of ethnic groups. An example of racism reported by Te Karere (Māori news programme) was a fictitious Facebook profile page that depicted a Māori "family obsessed with boozing, smoking dope and bashing women" (Te Karere NZ, 2013). The account had stolen the identity of Kimiora Webster, a secondary teacher at Rotorua Boys' High School, alongside a number of photos of other Māori identities. The page received over 58,000 likes and actively engaged its audience by posts that racialized Māori as criminals. While Webster and many other Māori made complaints about the page, at the time of reporting he had not received any response from Facebook and the false portrayal still remained accessible online. The lack of response from Facebook highlights the limited control and power users have in dealing with racial discrimination targeted through accounts and profiles created by others.

To further highlight this issue, while large social media corporations may project a position of neutrality, such a notion can hide racial discrimination. Lee (2007) discusses new forms of racism that exist within our society which do not overtly claim a hierarchy of race they speak to cultural or ethnic differences. Lee states that, "Racism often escapes recognition as such, because hegemonic discourses have secured it for a new ideological transparency, enabling dominant groups to sustain racist constructions of social difference" (p. 31).

In 2012, groups of Indigenous people were shut out of their accounts when Facebook introduced a 'real-name' policy that attempted to close any accounts that appeared to have fictitious names. The policy was created after Facebook revealed that it had 83 million fake accounts, and experienced an immediate drop in its share price (The Guardian, 2014a). The real-name policy impacted on marginalized communities that included Indigenous groups, members of the LGBT stage performers and political activists, all of whom were denied access on the basis of their names being seen as fake. The Facebook's chief product officer, "affirmed that the 'real-name' policy is meant to differentiate from other parts of the internet that accept anonymity and to protect people from trolls and abuse conducted by those protected by anonymity" (The Guardian, 2014b). However, instead it clearly highlighted the discrimination that marginalized groups continue to experience within the online social media space.

Disruption of Indigenous Ways of Being

For Indigenous communities, cultural knowledge systems, ancestry and ways of operating as a collective are interwoven through one's Indigenous experiential physical existence. The internet can be seen as a way to distance Indigenous communities from one's natural connection to life (Iseke-Barnes & Danard, 2007). Howe (1998) supports this view in his article, Cyberspace is No Place for Tribalism, and warns of the dangers that the Internet poses for Indigenous groups. He describes the Internet as a global village, whereby the irrelevance between people and landscapes further displaces Indigenous communities who are connected spiritually to land. He highlights four key dimensions – spatial, social, spiritual and experiential – that are central to tribal life and community relationships. Howe also argues that these dimensions cannot be virtualized;

Tribalism must be practiced. It must be lived and experienced. It is not merely a way of thinking or some nebulous feeling, nor is it inherent in an individual's biological makeup. Tribalism requires full sensory interaction between tribal members, on the one hand, and between tribal communities and their surrounding environments, on the other hand. (Howe, 1998, p. 24)

Issues and tensions can arise when traditional cultural practices are shifted to the online space and are incongruous with cultural values. This is evident when social media provides an alternative space to grieve the loss of a person, when people find themselves unable to physically attend ceremonies.

O'Carroll (2013) raises a number of questions around Māori engaging in customary practices and accessing tribal knowledge through social media, rather than not physically returning their tribal lands. She highlights the issues for whānau around the tikanga of virtual spaces and the appropriateness of participating in tangihanga through social network sites. The postings of photographs of tupapaku and online videos of the tangi were seen by some as inappropriate and insensitive to the whānau of the deceased. While some of the participants in her study commented on the ability to say their goodbyes, create virtual memorials online and feel part of a tangihanga back home, other participants felt an inability to connect to the wairua of tangihanga. O'Carroll re-tells an experience shared by one of her participants:

...she kissed the computer screen to say goodbye to a deceased, and found it difficult to connect to the wairua of the deceased person. Her use of the term 'sad' in this instance was to signal the sense of the emptiness of this act compared with physical presence, as she felt removed from the experience of the tangihanga ritual. (O'Carroll, 2013, p. 211)

Such an example highlights how social media cannot take the place of face-to-face engagement in such situations. Cultural practices require a physical presence for people to experience fully and connect at a more spiritual and emotional level.

CONCLUSION

It is clear that social media can create a compelling space for Māori and Indigenous groups to connect in ways that support and reflect their Indigeneity. Indigenous groups are collectively engaging in social media to assert their tino rangatiratanga both at a local and global level. Social media is a powerful tool to galvanize political change, enabling large scale Indigenous movements to directly challenge Governments over the loss of tribal land rights. Additionally, social media has the potential to capture and revitalize Indigenous language and culture in ways that honors and sustains traditional knowledge and traditions.

Social media can also bring a number of risks for Māori and Indigenous communities by offering a new mode to perpetuate the dominant ideology and further the practice of colonization. As highlighted in this chapter, the misappropriation and exploitation of Indigenous culture and practices are amplified through the digitization and use of social media. It also highlights racial discrimination, as well as new forms of covert racism through the notion of neutrality. Finally, it looks at the disruption of Indigenous ways of being that draw upon the physical, emotional and spiritual self that cannot be replicated in the online environment.

This chapter highlights ways in which Māori and Indigenous groups are engaging in social media by drawing on Kaupapa Māori principles. Kaupapa Māori responds to the changing societal forces faced by Māori and the impact on our culture, aspirations and struggles in all sectors of society. This chapter also establishes the broader context for social media use by Indigenous groups which supports the next chapter's exploration of a Facebook group for Māori doctoral students and academics. While much work is still to be done in this area, it is intended that both chapters provided a way of thinking about ways in which the use of social media can contribute to the transformation of Māori and Indigenous people's cultural and educational aspirations.

REFERENCES

Alexander, C. J. (2010). International exploration of technology equity and the digital divide: Critical, historical and social perspectives. In P. Randolpleigh (Ed.), *From igloos to iPods: Inuit Qaujimajatuqangit and the internet in Canada* (pp. 80–105). IGI Global.

Bell, B. L., Budka, P., & Fiser, A. (2007). *"We were on the outside looking in": MyKnet. org: A First Nations online social network in Northern Ontario.* Presented at the 5th CRACIN Workshop, Montréal, Canada.

Belton, K. A. (2010). From cyberspace to offline communities: Indigenous peoples and global connectivity. *Alternatives, 35*(3), 193–215. doi:10.1177/030437541003500302

Carlson, B. (2013). The 'new frontier': Emergent Indigenous identities and social media. In M. Harris, M. Harris, & B. Carlson (Eds.), *The politics of identity: Emerging Indigeneity* (pp. 147–168). Sydney: University of Technology Sydney E-Press.

Carlson, B. L., Jones, L. V., Harris, M., Quezada, N., & Frazer, R. (2017). Trauma, shared recognition and Indigenous resistance on social media. *AJIS. Australasian Journal of Information Systems*, 21.

Dashper, M. G. (2017). *Te waha tieke: Exploring the educational potential of social networking environments for Māori students in northland schools* (Unpublished doctoral dissertation). The University of Auckland. ResearchSpace, Auckland, New Zealand. Retrieved from http://hdl.handle.net/2292/34400

Duarte, M. E. (2017). Connected activism: Indigenous uses of social media for shaping political change. *AJIS. Australasian Journal of Information Systems*, 21.

Farrell, A. C. (2017). Archiving the Aboriginal rainbow: Building an Aboriginal LGBTIQ portal. *AJIS. Australasian Journal of Information Systems*, 21.

Howe, C. (1998). Cyberspace is no place for tribalism. *Wicazo Sa Review*, *13*(2), 19. doi:10.2307/1409143

Huijser, H., & Bronnimann, J. (2014). Exploring the opportunities of social media to build knowledge in learner-centered Indigenous learning spaces. *Educating in Dialog: Constructing Meaning and Building Knowledge with Dialogic Technology*, *24*, 97–110.

Iseke, J., & Moore, S. (2011). Community-based indigenous digital storytelling with elders and youth. *American Indian Culture and Research Journal, 35*(4), 19–38. doi:10.17953/aicr.35.4.4588445552858866

Iseke-Barnes, J. (2002). Aboriginal and Indigenous people's resistance, the internet, and education. *Race, Ethnicity and Education*, *5*(2), 171–198. doi:10.1080/13613320220139617

Iseke-Barnes, J., & Danard, D. (2007). Indigenous knowledges and worldview: Representations and the Internet. *Information Technology and Indigenous People*, 27–29.

Keegan, T. T., Mato, P., & Ruru, S. (2015). Using Twitter in an Indigenous language: An analysis of te reo Māori tweets. *AlterNative: An International Journal of Indigenous Peoples, 11*(1), 59–75. doi:10.1177/117718011501100105

Keene, A. (2013, January 28). *Native appropriations*. Retrieved from http://nativeappropriations.com/2013/01/reflections-on-3-years-at-native-appropriations.html

Lee, J. (2008). *Ako: Pūrākau of Māori teachers' work in secondary schools* (Unpublished doctoral dissertation). The University of Auckland, New Zealand.

Lumby, B. (2010). Cyber-indigeneity: Urban indigenous identity on Facebook. *The Australian Journal of Indigenous Education, 39*(S1), 68–75. doi:10.1375/S1326011100001150

Mendelson, S. (2017, March). *Box Office: Disney's "Moana" sails past $600 million worldwide*. Retrieved from https://www.forbes.com/sites/scottmendelson/2017/03/16/box-office-disneys-moana-sails-past-600-million-worldwide/#65964eab43f7

Metge, J. (1995). *New growth from old: The whānau in the modern world*. Wellington: Victoria University Press.

Molyneaux, H., O'Donnell, S., Kakekaspan, C., Walmark, B., Budka, P., & Gibson, K. (2014). Social media in remote First Nation communities. *Canadian Journal of Communication, 39*(2), 275–288. doi:10.22230/cjc.2014v39n2a2619

Nakata, M. (2002). Indigenous knowledge and the cultural interface: Underlying issues at the intersection of knowledge and information systems. *IFLA Journal, 28*(5–6), 281–291. doi:10.1177/034003520202800513

O'Carroll, A. D. (2013). *Kanohi ki te kanohi-a thing of the past? An examination of Māori use of social networking sites and the implications for Māori culture and society* (Unpublished doctoral dissertation). Massey University, Palmerston North, New Zealand.

Parkhurst, N. D. (2017). Protecting oak flat: Narratives of survivance as observed through digital activism. *AJIS. Australasian Journal of Information Systems*, 21.

Petray, T. L. (2013). Self-writing a movement and contesting indigeneity: Being an Aboriginal activist on social media. Global Media Journal: Australian Edition, 7(1), 1–20.

Pihama, L. (2001). *Tihei mauri ora: Honouring our voices: Mana wahine as a Kaupapa Māori theoretical framework* (Unpublished doctoral dissertation). The University of Auckland. Research, New Zealand.

PihamaL. (2016a, January 1). Retrieved from https://www.facebook.com/leonie.pihama

PihamaL. (2016b, January 2). Retrieved from https://www.facebook.com/leonie.pihama

Pihama, L., & Cameron, N. (2012). Kua tupu te pā harakeke: Developing healthy whānau relationships. In *For Indigenous minds only: A decolonisation handbook* (pp. 231–244). School of Advanced Research.

Rotorua Daily Post. (2004, July 22). Retrieved from http://www.nzherald.co.nz/rotorua-daily-post/news/article.cfm?c_id=1503438&objectid=11297345

Smith, G. H. (1991). *Reform & Māori educational crisis: A grand illusion.* The University of Auckland.

Smith, G. H. (2003). *Indigenous struggle for the transformation of education and schooling. Keynote Address to the Alaska Federation of Natives (AFN)* Convention.

Smith, G. H. (2003). *Kaupapa Māori theory: Theorizing transformation of education and schooling.* Presented at the Kaupapa Māori Symposium, NZARE / AARE Joint Conference, Auckland, New Zealand. Retrieved from https://pdfs.semanticscholar.org/bc1e/df21dbdf7c94cf53c13d5d0c9b132f1102cb.pdf

Smith, L. T. (2003). *Decolonising methodologies: Research and Indigenous peoples* (6th ed.). Dunedin, New Zealand: University Otago Press.

SOUL - Save Our Unique Landscape Campaign. (n.d.). Retrieved November 3, 2017, from http://www.soulstopsha.org/

Te Karere, N. Z. (2013, June). *Outrage over Facebook pages depicting fake Māori family.* Retrieved from https://www.youtube.com/watch?v=uhekwe8-xh0

The Guardian. (2014a). *Facebook quarterly report reveals 83m profiles are fake.* Retrieved November 3, 2017, from https://www.theguardian.com/technology/2012/aug/02/facebook-83m-profiles-bogus-fake

The Guardian. (2014b). *Victory for drag queens as Facebook apologises for 'real-name' policy.* Retrieved November 3, 2017, from https://www.theguardian.com/technology/2014/oct/01/victory-drag-queens-facebook-apologises-real-name-policy

Tiakiwai, S., & Tiakiwai, H. (2008). *A literature review focused on virtual learning environments (VLEs) and e-Learning in the context of te reo Māori and Kaupapa Māori education.* Ministry of Education.

Virtanen, P. K. (2015). Indigenous social media practices in Southwestern Amazonia. *AlterNative: An International Journal of Indigenous Peoples, 11*(4), 350–362. doi:10.1177/117718011501100403

Waitoa, J. (2013). *E-whanaungatanga: The role of social media in Māori political engagement* (Unpublished Master's dissertation). Massey University, Palmerston North, New Zealand.

Waitoa, J., Scheyvens, R., & Warren, T. R. (2015). E-Whanaungatanga: The role of social media in Māori political empowerment. *AlterNative: An International Journal of Indigenous Peoples, 11*(1), 45–58. doi:10.1177/117718011501100104

APPENDIX

Please note, some of following Māori words are not direct translations, but explanations as they relate specifically to the context in which they are used in this chapter.

Ako: Culturally preferred pedagogy principle.
Aotearoa: New Zealand.
Hapū: Subtribe.
Iwi: Tribe.
Kaupapa Māori: Māori principles.
Pūrākau: Tribal stories.
Rangatahi: Youth.
Tamariki: Children.
Tangata Whenua: Local people.
Tangihanga: Funeral protocols.
Taonga Tuku Iho: The treasure and values that are inherited by us (cultural aspirations principle).
Te Karere: Māori news program.
Te Reo Māori: Māori language.
Tikanga: Protocols.
Tino Rangatiratanga: Self-determination principle.
Tupapaku: Deceased.
Tupuna: Ancestors.
Wairua: Spirit.
Whakapapa: Genealogy.
Whānau: Extended family.
Whanaungatanga: Relationship, kinship.

Chapter 4

A Kaupapa Māori Facebook Group for Māori and Indigenous Doctoral Scholars:
Maryann Lee in Conversation With Dr. Mera Lee-Penehira, Dr. Hinekura Smith, and Dr. Jennifer Martin

Maryann Lee
Unitec Institute of Technology, New Zealand

ABSTRACT

This chapter examines the use of Facebook to support Māori and Indigenous doctoral scholars who are enrolled in the MAI ki Tāmaki Makaurau doctoral programme in Auckland, New Zealand. The programme is part of a National Māori and Indigenous (MAI) Network aimed to increase doctoral participation and completion rates of Māori scholars. Drawing on three Kaupapa Māori principles introduced in chapter three: tino rangatiratanga (self-determination principle), taonga tuku iho (cultural aspirations principle), whānau (extended family structure principle), the author explores some of the key considerations in creating a Kaupapa Māori digital learning space with the use of social media. Through conversations with three Māori academics who adminisiter the MAI ki Tāmaki Facebook group, this chapter captuers their unique perspectives and provide rich insights into the ways in which the Facebook group can provide a strong network of support for Māori and Indigenous scholars.

DOI: 10.4018/978-1-5225-5826-2.ch004

INTRODUCTION

In 2012, the MAI ki Tāmaki Makaurau doctoral programme was led by Dr Jenny Lee-Morgan and Dr Mera Lee-Penehira at Te Puna Wānanga, School of Māori and Indigenous Education, the University of Auckland. The programme is part of a National Māori and Indigenous (MAI) Network, supported by Ngā Pae o te Maramatanga (Māori Centre of Research Excellence) primarily made up of Māori and Indigenous doctoral students and emerging academics enrolled in tertiary organisations throughout Aotearoa, New Zealand. Established in 2002, the Network aims to increase doctoral participation and completion rates of Māori scholars (Te Kupenga o MAI, n.d.). The MAI ki Tāmaki Makaurau doctoral programme was innovative in its approach, bringing Māori and Indigenous academics together through a range of cultural, social and academic events.

Alongside the MAI ki Tāmaki Makaurau programme a MAI ki Tāmaki Facebook Group was created to provide additional support and guidance for Māori scholars between events. Over the last six years the Facebook group's membership has steadily increased, with a total of 85 members in 2018. It has also extended its membership to include postgraduate Māori and Indigenous students, as well as senior Māori and Indigenous academics. The inclusion of Masters and Honors students is an important part of the recruitment or encouragement pathway into doctoral study, supporting a tuakana-teina approach (older and younger sibling relationship). Additionally, inviting senior academics to the Facebook group enables students to interact with a greater pool of Māori and Indigenous academic knowledge. The Facebook members are diverse in their research disciplines and research experiences, with a much higher ratio of Māori women (90%) to Māori men (10%).

This research examines how the MAI ki Tāmaki Facebook Group reflects a Kaupapa Māori online learning space to support Māori scholars on their doctoral journey. Through gaining perspectives from three senior Māori academics who administer the site - Dr Mera Lee-Penehira, Dr Jen Martin and Dr Hinekura Smith - this research seeks to identify key Kaupapa Māori elements that underpin the Facebook group, and highlight ways in which members engage with each other as Māori Indigenous academics.

This chapter is designed to be read in conjunction with chapter three, which provides a context for the use of social media for Indigenous communities in general. Chapter three highlights how Māori and Indigenous groups are engaging in social media in ways that reflect the cultural aspirations for their communities, as well as outlining the risks associated with social media. This chapter focuses on a case-study that examines the use of Facebook to support Māori and Indigenous students and academics within the New Zealand tertiary environment. Both chapters draw on three Kaupapa Māori principles to frame similar themes that were identified in the literature review and examples provided in chapter three, and in the case-study in this chapter.

A KAUPAPA MĀORI APPROACH

This research is underpinned by a Kaupapa Māori methodological approach outlined in chapter 3. Here, it is importan for the purpose of analyzing discussions about the Māori online space to reiterate key features of the approach, particular with regard to the role of the Kaupapa Māori researcher.

A Kaupapa Māori approach enables Māori researchers to engage from a local theoretical position and that encompasses a Māori worldview at a spiritual, cultural and political level (Smith, 2003). Kaupapa Māori seeks to legitimize cultural aspirations and identity and create a space for Māori to be Māori. Linda Smith (2003) describes Kaupapa Māori methodology as, "centering our concepts and world-views and then coming to know and understand theory and research from our own perspectives and for our own purposes" (p. 39).

Whilst Kaupapa Māori is intimately connected to the sustainability of Māori cultural identity and Māori knowledge, it has come from a political and strategic move to provide a powerful space for Māori researchers, and aligns with a critical theory paradigm that asserts a transformative praxis (Smith, 2012). Kaupapa Māori is considered to be a living response to the historical events of colonisation, and a resistance to the dominant power relationships that exist today (Walker, 1996). The term 'research' for Indigenous peoples can be a reminder of the historical colonisation practices carried out that saw Indigenous groups as the 'researched' (Waziyatawin & Yellow Bird, 2012).

With this in mind, Linda Smith (2003) argues that a critique of one's intention to conduct Kaupapa Māori research is essential. She proposes a series of questions that researchers must be mindful of: "Whose research is this? Who owns it? Whose interests does it serve? Who will benefit from it? Who has designed its questions and framed its scope? Who will write it up? How will the results be disseminated?" (p. 10). These questions assist Māori and Indigenous researchers to reflect upon their own research agenda, the responsibilities of being a researcher, and how their research may contribute directly to their communities, whānau, hapū and iwi (L. Smith, 2003).

RESEARCH METHOD

My research is a case-study on the MAI ki Tāmaki Facebook Group. I chose a case-study method as it enables the researcher to focus on, and capture in-depth perspectives of the three Māori academics who play an integral role in maintaining a digital space that supports Kaupapa Māori principles. This research is one example of a Māori and Indigenous Facebook group, and therefore is not intended to reflect and represent all Māori and Indigenous Facebook groups. However, the research does highlight some central principles that can be considered when using social media to develop a culturally safe digital learning space for Indigenous peoples.

My interest in this research stems back to an e-learning role I held at the Faculty of Education at the University of Auckland, New Zealand, where I supported teacher education lecturers to design online courses and integrate learning technologies in their teaching. I was fortunate to have the opportunity to work alongside Māori staff and doctoral students, and this work included supporting the MAI ki Tāmaki Programme in 2012. At the same time, I was undergoing my post-graduate studies in Māori education and developing an awareness of Kaupapa Māori theory and methodology. Through my studies I began to reflect more deeply on my identity as an Indigenous Māori Chinese woman growing up in a predominantly western world. In the process of applying a Kaupapa Māori lens to my research, I began to consider the impact of colonization on Indigenous communities, and how the Internet and digital technologies can play a role in perpetuating colonized ideologies and frameworks. I completed my Masters of Professional Studies in Education in 2015, focusing my research on how Māori tertiary students engage in digital learning spaces.

As a Kaupapa Māori researcher, developing relationships with the research participants and identifying with them is an important Kaupapa Māori principle. Indigenous researchers take on a 'participatory mode' whereby they, too, contribute their personal knowledge and understandings as part of the research process (Denzin & Lincoln, 2008). I am fortunate to have established relationships with all three participants over a number of years through various connections both within a whānau (family) and a professional context. At the time of interviewing, all participants worked at the University of Auckland in Māori academic positions. In this section, I introduce each of the participants.

Dr Mera Lee-Penehira (Iwi: Ngati Raukawa and Rangitaane) works as a senior Māori lecturer and Supervisor at Te Puna Wānanga, School of Māori and Indigenous Education at the Faculty of Education. Mera is also the Director of Research and Postgraduate Studies, offering support to Māori postgraduate and doctoral students. She is the academic leader for MAI ki Tāmaki Makaurau programme and established the MAI ki Tāmaki Facebook Group. Mera's research interests are on Māori and Indigenous women, identity and wellbeing. They include Māori sexual health and reproductive health, and she developed a Kaupapa Māori model of resistance and wellbeing in this context. Mera's doctoral research centred on traditional knowledge and healing practices case studying Māori women with hepatitis C. In particular, she examined the process of moko (traditional Māori skin carving) and notions of mouri as legitimate components of Māori wellbeing.

Dr Hinekura Smith (Iwi: Te Rarawa) is currently working at the Centre for Learning and Research in Higher Education, as a Māori Academic Developer. Previously, she taught as a Te Reo Māori teacher for many years in mainstream secondary schools, working with a wide range of youth, their whānau and communities. Hinekura has recently completed her Ph.D. and has been an active member of the Facebook group, initially as a doctoral student and now as an administrator. Hinekura's research explores Māori aspirations to live 'as Māori', through the stories of eight Māori women and the aspirations they hold for their children and grandchildren to live 'as Māori'.

Dr Jen Martin (Iwi: Te Rarawa) has a background in Māori immersion education. Jen is currently working as a lecturer of Te Reo Māori in Māori Studies, in the Faculty of Arts. Jen has also been an active member of the Facebook group and continues to support it as an administrator. Jen's research interests include Māori language revitalization and development, academic writing in Te Reo Māori (Māori language), and Māori achievement and advancement through education. Her doctoral thesis awarded in 2014, written in Te Reo, uses a Kaupapa Māori narrative research approach to consider the notion of educational success in the context of Kura Kaupapa Māori (Māori schooling).

All three participants bring a wealth of knowledge and experience as Kaupapa Māori academics, alongside the many other roles they play within their whanau (family), hapū (sub-tribe) and Iwi (tribe). During my interviews, I was mindful of my role and responsibilities as researcher, and that my engagement with each of the participants was underpinned by the following values:

- Aroha ki te tangata (a respect for people),
- Kanohi kitea ('the seen face', which refers to presenting yourself to people face to face),
- Titiro, whakarongo ... korero (look, listen ... speak),
- Manaaki ki te tangata (share and host people, be generous),
- Kia tupato (be cautious),
- Kaua e takahi te mana o te tangata (do not trample over the mana of people),
- Kaua e mahaki (don't flaunt your knowledge). (L. Smith, 2003, p. 120)

Ethics approval was sought and approved by Unitec Institute of Technology in 2017. In accordance with ethical requirements, participants were provided with information outlining the aims of the research along with individual consent forms.

MAI DOCTORAL PROGRAMME

Under the leadership of Professors Graham and Linda Smith, the initiative for a doctoral network originally began in the 1990s during their time teaching and mentoring Māori postgraduate students at the University of Auckland. Graham and Linda had a vision for a national Māori network for postgraduate students that transitioned and supported Māori and Indigenous scholars in their doctoral studies. The conscious move to increase the number of Māori doctoral students and develop a national network was supported by Ngā Pae o te Māramatanga (Māori Centre of Research Excellence). In 2002, the MAI programme across six regions was funded, and included ten MAI networks groups throughout New Zealand.

The key objectives for the MAI programme aim to: increase Māori doctoral participation and completion rates; grow a strong network of Māori researchers across New Zealand; support pathways from post-graduate to doctoral studies; and to build Māori leadership and research capability from doctoral study to post-doctoral research and to future career pathways (Te Kupenga o MAI, n.d.). Each network offers different activities, such as academic seminars, Indigenous conferences, writing retreats and workshops and social gatherings. Despite such a highly regarded programme, recent restructuring of funding has meant that programs are now having to severely limit the activities being offered.

The MAI programme has been instrumental in building a strong network for Māori scholars to regularly come together in both a culturally and academic supportive forum. Between 2005 and 2015 the number of doctoral students have almost doubled, with 275 doctoral students enrolled in 2005, and 515 enrolled in 2015. While these figures highlight the success of the support provided by MAI, Māori-awarded doctorates are still underrepresented, making up only 6% of all New Zealand doctorates awarded between 2006 and 2013 (Pihama, et al., 2017, p. 29).

Research highlights a number of challenges for Māori and Indigenous scholars during their doctoral journey. These include: lack of institutional support, limited access to Māori academics and supervisors, and feelings of isolation within their disciplines (Hohepa, 2010; McKinley, Grant, Middleton, Irwin, & Williams, 2007). A recent report titled Te Tātua o Kahukura (2017) identifies similar challenges that include both systemic issues and financial constraints. The report highlights how doctoral Māori students felt that mainstream activities were often not appropriate, and that "institutional racism and white privilege were identified as a fundamental issue for Māori and Indigenous doctoral scholars engaging in western university structures" (Pihama et al., 2017, p. 8).

MAI KI TĀMAKI FACEBOOK GROUP

The following section highlights some of the key themes identified from the interviews with three Māori academics who administiter the MAI ki Tāmaki Facebook group. Their perspectives provide a rich insight into the ways in which the Facebook group can support Māori and Indigenous scholars, as well highlighting the considerations in creating a Kaupapa Māori digital learning space. I have drawn on three of the Kaupapa Māori principles by G. Smith (1991), to reflect a range of research themes; Tino rangatiratanga (self-determination principle), Taonga tuku iho (cultural aspirations principle), Whānau (extended family structure principle). Each of these principles have been explored in chapter three and provide a cultural context for the following section.

Tino Rangatiratanga: Self-Determination Principle

'Tino rangatiratanga' represents sovereignty and self-determination for Māori whānau, hapū and iwi. It can also be viewed as a direct protest to the Crown that acknowledges the struggles over Māori sovereignty and the loss of control by tangata whenua. Tino rangatiratanga is reflected within the Facebook group in a number ways. Mera highlights how members are given the power to equally contribute in ways that supports the collective group which supports the principle of tino rangatiratanga. She discusses how the Facebook group has been intentionally set up without an approval or editing function by the administrators to control the space:

Anyone can post up what they like - there is no approval function on that page ... that's an important underpinning of the page - I think this is something that is connected to a Kaupapa Māori way of doing things in social media. Because it takes away that power relationship between the administrator and participant. We all have equal value and opportunity and power to put things up there.

Additionally, Mera discusses how the Facebook group reflects a strong political element supporting the Kaupapa Māori principle of tino rangatiratanga. Raising the political awareness of Māori scholars is something that Mera sees as one of her roles as the MAI programme leader and a senior Māori academic:

I think that one of our jobs in the MAI programme is to build and maintain a sound level of political awareness and consciousness. Part of the underpinning of the MAI programme is that you can't really be a successful Māori or Indigenous scholar without a clear understanding of politics and without strong politics to your academic work. The MAI ki Tāmaki Makaurau programme encourages and helps people develop that, and the Facebook page certainly reflects this - we have some pretty political posts that happen in our group.... Scrolling through the page, I can see that it is really highly political. And I don't think postgraduate pakeha sites are highly political. I'm on one of them here at the university and they are more about informing events, academic workshops and things happening. We do all of that - but we also politicize quite strongly through this medium.

For Mera, the Facebook group is an effective forum for raising the political conscientization of Māori scholars at both a local and global scale. It also connects students, particulary who may be experiencing isolation in their doctoral journey, to a wider Indigenous community, and a greater awareness of Indigenous political movements throughout the world.

It's all about political conscientization, doing research that is necessarily transformative for whānau, hapū and iwi. When we see things that are happening in the wider Aotearoa or the wider world that are transformative, that reflect those kinds of values we are trying to promote in the MAI programme, then we pop those up in the Facebook group. And it's a good way of beginning to connect people with other Indigenous and native scholars throughout the world, which really excites people......Our politics can be quite burdensome, and to see the work that other people are doing like in Canada Hawaii or in Australia is sometimes quite heartening and strengthening of our own work that we need to do here. It can be just a matter of seeing a Facebook post that pushes you through the next part of the chapter and your work, and it reminds you that your work is absolutely and fundamentally linked to bigger things than this piece of study. That it is linked to global Indigenous and Native activism. It just gives people that wider lens outside of the supervision relationship, where you are quite focused on that chapter.

Mera's comments provide insight into how significant the principle of tino rangatiratanga is in the lives and work of Māori academics, and how this is also strongly reflected within the Facebook group. The MAI ki Tāmaki Facebook Group provides a powerful space to raise the level of political conscientization of Māori academics, to demonstrate political activism and to connect them to a wider Indigenous community.

Taonga Tuku Iho: Cultural Aspirations Principle

'Taonga tuku iho' is a key Kaupapa Māori principle that validates Māori ways of being and creates a space for Māori to 'be Māori', whereby cultural aspirations and identity are legitimized. In chapter three, the section on taonga tuku iho highlighted ways in which Indigenous people engage in social media to support their cultural aspirations. This section discusses the online tikanga of the Facebook group and the creation of a culturally safe space for Māori academics within which to engage.

My discussion with Hinekura led us to explore the online tikanga (protocols) of the Facebook group. For Māori, tikanga is about ways of conducting oneself that is considered tika or correct in ways that draw upon on Māori principles and values. Hinekura begins by discussing the online tikanga for accepting members into the group and draws on the principle of whanaungatanga (maintaining relationships) that places emphasis on people's established connections and relationships.

At the moment, someone will request to join, and they might sit there for a while, whilst we find out who they are and how they were invited into the Facebook group. Our process is inclusive - but we also need to understand that whanaungatanga comes about through connections - and if we've got requests from people we don't know, then we need to establish where the relationship lies within the group.

Hinekura emphasizes the importance of knowing where the connection lies with new members, so that there is a shared responsibility and obligation in inviting members into the group.

When I think of whakapapa in that digital space - it goes back to who brought that person in, and so where is that connection. It hasn't happened as far as I can recall, but if there was something really inappropriate put up on the Facebook group - it would be a matter of tracing back to who brought that person here. That's the responsibility of introducing someone into that whakapapa, which I think is a very Māori thing.

Hinekura reflects on how the tikanga of the group is not explicitly outlined anywhere on the Facebook group. However, there is an assumption that members should know how to conduct themselves within a Kaupapa Māori framework. She conceptualizes the Facebook group as a space that supports Māori values and principles, and draws parallels with a physical Māori space.

When you go into a Māori space, you sit back and watch what's happening and what's the norm. Is it ok to do this? and can I sit here? Perhaps that is a similar way of operating in this digital space. When I am invited into the Facebook group, I sit back and I read and watch how others operate first before posting. So just like when we go into the marae ... there's not a written set of guidelines ..... If there was an occasion where there was something not right, like at a marae when someone sits in the wrong place, or if someone wears their shoes in the whare, then we have a conversation, and a bit of leaning in and support of that person.

When asking Hinekura whether Māori values could be expressed and experienced within an online space, she felt that they were present within the MAI ki Tāmaki Facebook Group.

The idea of whanaungatanga (relationships) and manaakitanga (caring for each othe) are important to how we support each other. Whether it's sitting here like we are now, or whether it's an online discussion on Facebook. Would somebody mind reading this chapter and giving feedback? So koha-atu-koha mai (reciprocity) is also important. And just a whole lot of aroha (love).

The values expressed by Hinekura contribute to a Kaupapa Māori space where being Māori is 'normalized'. Additionally Jen highlights the importance of incorporating the Māori language in her posts, and describes how it validates students as Māori within the online learning space.

On a Māori Facebook page, things Māori are much more normal. You are not going to be looked upon as holding extreme views, nor are you expected to clarify or explain certain things further..... because it is much more accepted and it's much more normal. And you can share things in a Māori group and not question yourself about how are non-Māori going to respond to these comments? ....Posting in Te Reo (Māori language) is a big deal for me, we are a predominantly Māori group, we are a Kaupapa Māori group - so why not post in both languages. I do always try and post bilingually. As someone who wrote in Māori for my PHD, I think it is important to continue promoting the use of te reo Māori in academic spaces as it is becoming more common for people to engage in academic writing in te reo Māori. However, I do keep the posts bilingual knowing that there are also many of our people who wouldn't necessarily understand if I just post in Māori.

Mera also talks about how the MAI ki Tāmaki Facebook Group provides members with a culturally safe space to express themselves. She discusses how members will often share their challenges and demands that reflect their doctoral journeys. Mera highlights how these are not limited just to research challenges that students face, but the wider issues that impact on their lives:

I think they see MAI Ki Tāmaki group is a space where they can discuss not just the academic challenges they are facing but the broader challenges in terms of - managing doctoral life, whānau life, hapū life, iwi life, the whole socio economic political environment that we are all living. I think that as a cohort the programme provides for that and that is reflected on the Facebook page and in the posts..... People will post things like a picture of themselves balancing a baby in one hand and the other hand on the keyboard laptop. They are commenting, "Here I am up till mid-night typing up the last draft of chapter 3, wouldn't have it any other way holding my baby." Those sorts of posts serve to strengthen the cohort - people are sharing the realities of being a mum or dad, and having children, doing a doctorate and working.

The principle of taonga tuku iho was highlighted at the beginning of this section by discussing the tikanga of the Facebook group that is supported by Māori values and principles. The notion of whanaungatanga provided a premise for the group membership, and ensured a strong sense of obligation and expectation in relation to how members conducted themselves online. Creating a space that felt culturally safe and that normalized 'being Māori' was another key component of this section. Supporting Te Reo Māori use in the site, and encouraging members to share their doctoral experiences all contributed to a Facebook group that underpins a Kaupapa Māori approach.

Whānau: Extended Family Structure Principle

The term 'whānau' is often used as way to describe a group of people who share the same kaupapa or are working together to a shared outcome. The practice of whanaungatanga comes from whānau, which places emphasis on strong relationships amongst members, and the roles and obligations of all members.

The MAI ki Tāmaki Makaurau programme operates as a whānau and, as highlighted in the first section, whanaungatanga underpins both the programme and the Facebook group. Jen discusses how the administrators manage the group in an inclusive way, and how it has extended its membership to include post-graduate students and other Māori and Indigenous academics. One of the aims of the MAI ki Tāmaki Makaurau programme is to encourage postgraduate students to transition to doctoral studies, and Jen sees the Facebook group as an effective platform for this:

In the past couple of years, we've tried to extend our reach .... One of the things we are trying to do is not only support those that are currently doing their PhDs, but to try and show those who are at honors or masters level that there is a pathway. For many of them it is a massive decision for them to go into a PhD.... It's a good way for them to be able to engage and interact with others that might already be on that journey and to get a feel for the sorts of things people are going through.

Jen describes how, within the Facebook group, various members will take on different roles to support other members, so that it is not always left to the administrators and senior academics to provide assistance. She discusses the concept of 'tuakana-teina' within the Facebook group, where members within the group, particularly those who are closer to the completion of their doctorate, are providing greater guidance to those starting their academic journey:

Whether we are finished our PHDs, whether we are just starting - we all have something to learn from everybody else in the group. Whether it's people posting about their research or sharing an opinion about something - we can learn from each other - so just being part of the group, and being in that collegial and scholarly environment is an opportunity to learn constantly, even if some are more active than others ...... We have whanaungatanga as a core principle in everything that we do. Trying to include everybody, trying to encourage participation from everybody. But also, the tuakana-teina approach, where there are those who may be finished or closer to the end who may be able to support those coming through.

The Facebook group has a number of senior Māori academics, professors and supervisors as members. All administrators discuss the value of having senior academics joining the group to extend their support to doctoral scholars, as well as members providing support to each other. Mera states:

If you think about the underpinning of ako being that notion of reciprocity and people contributing and sharing to each other's growth, it's very much a part of what MAI programme is about, and you can see that evident on the Facebook page as well ..... It's great opportunity for students to engage with professors in an environment that is less threatening. They are getting lots of mentorship from people like myself Jenny and Leonie who are senior academics who engage on that page, but also there's peer mentoring that goes on. Particularly between the third, fourth, fifth year doctoral candidates and those that just come in.

Another key concept that was discussed by all administrators was the significance of 'kanohi-ki-te-kanohi', the ability for members to engage face-to-face. All administrators felt that the Facebook group complemented the face-to-face space, and that it was the physical engagement amongst members that was critical to the success of the Facebook group. Mera states:

The real growth for our doctoral students are those who engage in both the face-to-face end of the programme and the social media scene. People don't see the Facebook page as an alternative to the face-to-face engagement-they see it as an entry into the face-to-face, or backing up the face-to-face stuff. So, we have opportunities to meet monthly and Facebook is used in the between times.

Jen reflects on the MAI ki Tāmaki Makaurau writing retreats that she has attended with other Māori doctoral students, and feels that many of the conversations shared could not have occurred in the online space.

The online group helped us maintain relationships outside of those face-to-face meetings. But if we didn't have any face-to-face interaction then we are just not going to interact in the same manner as on the Facebook group. The two spaces complement each other.

Hinekura also reflects on the physical engagement with another person compared to engaging in the Facebook group. She highlights how the online space cannot replicate the physical space, particularly in relation to the wairua and the spiritual breath of a person:

In a physical connection, you have the wairua there. That is the risk of the online space - how does the wairua of our korero come through? Ko te Ha - the spiritual breath of the person - that you can't just send through the keyboard and Te Ao Hurihuri.

When further considering the online space, Hinekura suggests that wairua (spirit of a person) can potentially be felt within the site, but this is dependent on whether or not you have met that person in the physical sense before:

There is some wairua in the site - I wonder if the key to that is that the fact that we have real live relationships with these people. When we know that person, how they operate and how they talk - we are better able to interpret and feel their wairua. If I didn't know a person in a physical way - would I understand and feel what they are posting? I don't think so.

This section discusses ways in which the Facebook group operates as a whānau in terms of supporting a collective kaupapa. The notion of ako is fundamental to the Facebook group, where reciprocity is central to how members support each other and take on roles and responsibilities for the good of the group. The Kaupapa Māori learning environment draws from the principle of kanohi-ki-te-kanohi principles that enables students to connect, in ways that are not able to be replicated online.

CONCLUSION

This chapter provides a case-study on the MAI ki Tāmaki Facebook Group and highlights key themes that were discussed by the administrators. A strong emphasis in the research was to examine the Kaupapa Māori elements that underpin the Facebook group, which enable Māori doctoral scholars and academics to engage in ways that support their cultural values and practices.

For administrators, it is critical to create a space where being Māori is 'normalized', and where principles, such as whanaungatanga, manaakitanga, and aroha contribute to this. Additionally, a strong sense of reciprocity amongst the group is expected, ensuring that there is a responsibility to the collective by all members. While the Facebook group was clearly not a substitute or a replication of a Māori physical space, some aspects of the online space could be conceptualized in the same way, particularly when it came to tikanga and ways of engaging within the group.

Emphasis on establishing relationships in a physical space through kanohi-ki-te-kanohi was of high importance. Administrators felt that without this face-to-face engagement the relationships within the online forum would lack a sense of whanaungatanga, as well as wairua that could be felt only between members with a prior physical connection. The Facebook group was a valuable place to continue and extend conversations that were had during MAI-ki-Tāmaki programme events. It also provided a space to raise political conscientization amongst scholars and opportunities to be more connected to Indigenous communities at a global level.

A central aspiration for the MAI ki Tāmaki Makaurau programme is for Māori and Indigenous scholars to remain grounded and connected to whānau, hapū, iwi and communities, and to engage in research that purposefully seeks to contribute to the positive development and transformation of their communities. This research indicates that the MAI ki Tāmaki Facebook Group provides a new platform to support this aspiration in ways that align with a Kaupapa Māori framework. The use of social media sites, if managed by and for Māori, can become culturally safe places for learning in ways that reflects their cultural practices and values.

REFERENCES

Denzin, N. K., & Lincoln, Y. S. (2008). Critical methodologies and Indigenous inquiry. In *Handbook of critical methodologies and Indigenous inquiry* (pp. 1–20). Sage Publications.

Hohepa, M. (2010). 'Doctoring' our own: Confessions of a Māori doctoral supervisor. In J. Jesson, V.M. Carpenter, M. McLean, M. Stephenson & Airini (Eds.), University teaching reconsidered: justice, practice, inquiry (pp. 129-138). Wellington, New Zealand: Dunmore Publishing Ltd.

McKinley, E., Grant, B., Middleton, S., Irwin, K., & Williams, L. R. T. (2007). Teaching and learning in the supervision of Māori Doctoral Students: Project outline. *MAI Review LW, 1*(3), 6.

Pihama, L., Lee-Morgan, J., Tiakiwai, S., Tauroa, T., Mahuika, R., & Lonebear, D. (2017). *Te Tātua o Kahukura.* Te Kotahi Research Institute.

Smith, G. (2012). Interview: Kaupapa Māori: The dangers of domestication. *New Zealand Journal of Educational Studies*, 47, 10–20.

Smith, G. H. (1991). *Reform & Māori educational crisis: A grand illusion.* The University of Auckland.

Smith, L. T. (2003). *Decolonising methodologies: Research and Indigenous peoples* (6th ed.). Dunedin, New Zealand: University Otago Press.

Te Kupenga o MAI. (n.d.). *Te Kupenga o MAI Māori and Indigenous Scholar Support*. Retrieved November 6, 2017, http://mai.ac.nz/about

Walker, S. (1996). *Kia tau te rangimarie: Kaupapa Māori theory as a resistance against the construction of Māori as the other* (Unpublished master's thesis). The University of Auckland, New Zealand.

Waziyatawin, & Yellow Bird, M. (Eds.). (2012). *For indigenous minds only: A decolonization handbook*. School for Advanced Research Press.

APPENDIX

Please note, some of following Māori words are not direct translations, but explanations as they relate specifically to the context in which they are used in this chapter.

Ako: Culturally preferred pedagogy principle.
Aotearoa: New Zealand.
Aroha: Love.
Aroha ki te Tangata: A respect for people.
Hapū: Subtribe.
Iwi: Tribe.
Kanohi Kitea: "The seen face," which refers to presenting yourself to people face to face.
Kanohi-ki-te-Kanohi: Face-to-face.
Kaua e Mahaki: Do not flaunt your knowledge.
Kaua e Takahi te Mana o te Tangata: Do not trample over the mana of people.
Kaupapa: Collective philosophy.
Kaupapa Māori: Māori principles.
Kia Piki Ake i Ngā Raruraru o te Kainga: The mediation of socio-economic factors principle.
Kia Tupato: Be cautious.
Ko te Ha: The essence of life.
Koha-Atu-Koha Mai: Reciprocity.
MAI Ki Tāmaki Makaurau: Auckalnd Māori and Indigenous doctoral program.
Manaaki Ki Te Tangata: Share and host people, be generous.
Manaakitanga: Kindness and caring.
Rangatahi: Youth.
Tamariki: Children.
Tangata Whenua: Local people.
Taonga Tuku Iho: The treasure and values that are inherited by us (cultural aspirations principle).
Te Ao Hurihuri: The changing world.
Te Reo Māori: Māori language.
Tikanga: Protocols.

Tika: Correct.
Tino Rangatiratanga: Self determination principle.
Titiro, Whakarongo ... Korero: Look, listen ... speak.
Tuakana-Teina: Older younger sibling relationship.
Wairua: Spirit.
Whakapapa: Genealogy.
Whānau: Extended family.
Whanaungatanga: Relationship, kinship.

Chapter 5

Using Social Media in Creating and Implementing Educational Practices

Robyn Gandell
Unitec Institute of Technology, New Zealand

Inna Piven
Unitec Institute of Technology, New Zealand

ABSTRACT

Social media use has become ubiquitous in the everyday lives of many people around the world. Combined with smartphones, these interactive websites provide a vast array of new activities and immediate access to a world of information for both teachers and students. Research into the use of social media in educational practice is growing. In this chapter, the authors examine the use of social media from the perspective of lecturers and learning designers in a tertiary education institute in New Zealand. Data from a qualitative, interview-based research investigation highlights three key themes: 1) the use of social media as a course management tool; 2) the use of social media to enhance student centered learning; and 3) the need for institutional support for using social media in educational contexts.

INTRODUCTION

Over the last twenty years social media websites, particularly commercial social media sites, have increased in number and functionality (Tess, 2013; Chaffey, 2017). This has happened as, and perhaps because of, developments

DOI: 10.4018/978-1-5225-5826-2.ch005

in smartphone technology where millions of people now have everyday access to handheld computers and an increasing array of applications (Smith, 2010). Using smartphones, it is now possible to easily record, edit and post photos, videos and other media to social media sites where they can be viewed, potentially by millions of people but more likely by friends and relatives. With such large numbers of people worldwide interacting through social media sites everyday (Chaffey, 2017), social interactions are changing and this has the potential for significant change in classroom social interactions as well. The early reaction of many lecturers and teachers to mobile phones was to ban use of these devices in the classroom. As smartphones evolved, educators and institutions realized that these devices allowed unprecedented access to information and to the world from the classroom. In addition, with the growth of online Learning Management Systems (LMS) and blended learning in education, some educators realized that social media could also offer a way to enhance the learning and teaching in the classroom.

Although there is a growing body of literature on social media, the research into the benefits and challenges for tertiary learning is still emerging (Salmon, 2015; Tess, 2013). This research provides a snapshot of lecturers' and learning designers' use of social media platforms in a tertiary education context. The study investigates the experiences of these educators, their use of social media in learning and teaching, and their understanding of how social media fits within a pedagogical framework and best teaching practices. In seeking to understand what is happening in these courses from a lecturer's and learning designer's perspective we posed the following research question:

How is social media effectively integrated in learning design and development within the tertiary educational context?

BACKGROUND

Social media is a new social and cultural reality characterized by unlimited opportunities for connection, communication, information seeking and knowledge sharing. As Piven and Breazeale (2016) state; "the most noticeable changes in all aspects of our collective, private and public lives are connected to the emergence of social media" (p. 283). In a multitude of ways, social media plays an important role in day-to-day practices and experiences within the education sector. For example, the recent global survey of higher education social media usage by Hootsuite (2017) reported that over 90%

of education providers across the globe are now engaged with social media. While marketing and communication departments remain the most common users, there is a high adaption of social media by academic staff as well. The report also confirms that a changing student profile is the key driver behind social media adaptation by educators. As Benson (2016) states, "this new generation of students has provoked the proliferation of technology resources that could be used by academic staff to facilitate students' learning experience" (as cited in Kofinas, Al-Shawakbeh, & Lim, 2016, p. 268).

Indeed, in the past ten years, institutions, teachers and learning designers have become increasingly aware of the possibilities offered by social media for learning and teaching. If used appropriately, some researchers report, social media can lead students to more effective self-directed learning (McLoughlin & Lee, 2010; Salmon et al, 2015), better communication and collaborative skills (Rambe, 2012), and development of educational communities (Bosch, 2009). Griesemer believes that social media can help to improve students' learning experiences by preparing them "to enter a workforce that is not geographically constrained... and have highly developed online collaboration skills" (Griesemer, 2012, p. 9).

In response to ongoing technological development and challenges associated with a "mobile society" (Samovar & Porter, 2003, p. 1), educators have begun to take social media seriously and attempted to implement new teaching approaches or redesign existing ones. However, academic research into the meaning of these new approaches, and their possible implications for learning processes, course design and delivery, is still emerging. Moreover, some studies reveal mixed findings on the place of social media in education. Nonetheless, Hootsuite's global survey shows that the number one goal for tertiary education for 2018 is to develop a clear social media strategy. At this point, given social media's role in society, there is a need for academic research into the concrete teaching practices of, and experiences with, the use of social media to understand its implications for tertiary education. This study intends to contribute to that understanding.

METHODOLOGY

The study follows a grounded theory methodology, in which knowledge and ideas are understood to develop from social interaction and personal experiences (Corbin & Strauss, 2015). The world, and the knowledge in the world, is seen as ever changing so that understanding the world requires analyzing the way people interact and construct knowledge (Corbin & Strauss, 2015). To understand the use of social media in tertiary education the authors, therefore, needed to explore tertiary educators experiences in using social media in their personal learning and teaching, actions and interactions.

In this research, qualitative interviews are employed to explore lecturers' and learning designers' experiences in creating and implementing educational practices using social media. This method allows for investigation into the current use of social media in learning and teaching from the perspective of those using these social media tools in the tertiary context. The outcomes of these interviews are analyzed thematically to uncover key themes. The authors also use these interviews to examine best practices in the practical use of social media in blended learning in tertiary education contexts.

Grounded theory rejects notions of a universal truth and researchers certainly recognize that this research does not provide universality in the results. However, the authors hope this research provides some insight into the state of learning and teaching using social media that can be further explored. In addition, the authors acknowledge that research approaches of individual researchers (ranging from participant interviews to researcher transcription and analysis) are influenced by the researchers' own perspectives. To minimize this influence, the authors, use a variety of methods including using the independent analysis by two researchers, rechecking the analysis with interviewees and self-reflection on the analysis.

The five participants selected for interview were chosen from educationalists in a single tertiary institute in New Zealand. This institute provides programs from pre-degree to master's thesis study including vocational programs, certificate, diploma and degree qualifications in a variety of disciplines. The participants were lecturers and course developers who had been engaged in tertiary teaching for at least five years, although some had been teaching for much longer and at different tertiary institutions. All had used a variety of social media platforms in their teaching and course development; one participant for more than two years and the other four participants for over five years. Participants taught not only in different programs such as business, bridging education, sport and education, but also in courses from pre-degree to master's levels, and usually across several of these levels. One participant had taught in pre-degree, degree and masters programs. Three of the participants were female and two were male with their ages ranging from 35-55 years of age. The researchers acknowledge that using five participants is not a representative sample. However, the varied background of the participants enabled researchers to gather a wide variety of responses from these educationalists and thus a better understanding of the uses of social media in a tertiary context. Ethics approval was sought from the participants' tertiary institution and participants were invited to take part in the research. Prior to interviews, informed consent was gained from all participants.

From each individual participant interview transcription, the researchers extracted and gathered together evolving units of meaning. These units of meaning were then collated into emerging themes and compared across all of the participant interviews. These themes were clustered into categories across participant interviews from which three key themes emerged: 1) social media as a classroom management tool; 2) social media as an enabler of student-centered teaching practice; and 3) institutional support and management issues related to social media use in teaching.

DATA ANALYSIS AND KEY THEMES

Theme 1: Social Media as a Course Management Tool

The first key theme to emerge from this study identifies that although social media gained acceptance and a "spotlight" role in education as "a shift towards new... subject formation" and "collaborative modes of enquiry" (Hemmi, Bayne, & Landt, 2009, p. 29), first and foremost it is perceived by many educators as a course management tool. In this regard, a wide array of different aspects of course management have been identified and grouped around the theme defined as "social media as a course management tool".

Social media as a course management tool refers to the extent to which social media has been effectively integrated into course design and delivery. There are several relevant categories that emerged during the data analysis:

- Aligning social media with course learning outcomes
- Reinforcing student engagement & monitoring study progress
- Setting course rules and expectations
- Managing course information & student access to course materials
- Facilitating group collaboration

Aligning Social Media Use With Course Learning Outcomes

In the discussion of the application of social media to course design, participants point to learning outcomes as one of the deciding factors and defining components for course organization, delivery and activities:

We made sure that every week we would be saying to students – we have got these questions [on Facebook] and they are aligning to these learning outcomes.

I have 5 learning outcomes and 13 weeks to teach. When I look at the course calendar I try to identify the best way to use social media.

A part of the learning outcomes is communication and how you work within a team and engagement, this includes a FB group.

However, the focus on the alignment between course learning outcomes and social media is more an exception than a common practice. Participants note that the changes they implemented to course design were not necessarily driven by learning outcomes or specific pedagogical approaches:

We didn't have any real infrastructure...I do think that pedagogy still needs to occur and part of that is to make sure it is in alignment with learning outcomes, assessments and graduate profile.

We set up [Facebook group] very quickly. We don't have any measurements. A lot of the time with new staff we are just kind of muddling along with what works for now.

The examples above indicate that participants tend to emphasize the practical rationality of using social media in course delivery, rather than a required pedagogy for new learning environments. In this respect, McLoughlin & Lee (2010) note that "teachers who adapt social software tools should not do so merely to appear conversant with the tools, but to ensure integration of the tools with sound pedagogical strategies" (p. 38). Whether or not this integration can be achieved easily, a discussion is critical as there is an obvious need to make the learning processes not just manageable, but meaningful for students.

Reinforcing Student Engagement and Monitoring Study Progress

The responses provided by participants show that the decision to incorporate social media into course delivery is often motivated by "quite an honest reflection on students", specifically on their engagement with the course:

We were not happy with the engagement of students... And we tried to reframe the lecture to be more a conversation. Students can engage with the content before attending a lecture. So it was a bit of a change for the institution at this point.

According to the participants, social media provides distinct opportunities to design engaging and interactive courses. For example, one of the research participants learned that social media helped him and his colleague improve students' attendance. By posting course revision questions on Facebook, they were able to achieve a better attendance rate:

Every week we set a series of questions for students to reflect on, that are going to be answered during the next lecture. What we have noticed that for a number of students the attendance at a lecture was a little higher. We didn't publish the answers on Facebook. You have to come along next week to find out.

One participant who intensively uses Tumblr in her courses believes that social media makes it easier to keep track of student progress and provide timely feedback. The features of the social media platform enabled participants to see, for example, not only if assignments are completed but also the student's effort behind that assignment.

It also shows evidence of work, quantity, regularity, a variety [of students' posts] by using archive feature. [Students] cannot find excuses for not doing work. If students are not doing work, it is obvious. [You can] keep an eye on progress and you can support immediately.

The data also shows that some participants use specific social media features such as Facebook polls to check students' understanding of the course content:

We used a polling feature. We asked questions and provide a number of options and then see where students are sitting with that. An idea was... what is their prior knowledge coming to the session.

In a very general sense, social media can perform functions that are typically assigned to learning management systems. As Wang, Woo, Quek, Yang and Liu (2012) conclude, "the Facebook group can be used as LMS as it has certain pedagogical, social and technological affordances" (p. 428). However, determining the extent to which social media can be used as a supplement or even a substitute to a LMS is a difficult task and this is evident throughout the interview data. While participants recognize the limitations of the institutional LMS in terms of informal learning and communication, they feel that it is too early to give social media a central role in learning and teaching. As this research shows a LMS, such as Moodle, and social media can exist in parallel:

There was no connection between the two. It was a case of ...we are not going to use Moodle forums, our conversation will happen on FB instead... It [Facebook] is a really powerful connecting tool, which we can leverage to create a socially constructive type of learning.

This finding concurs with a study by Garmendía and Cobos (2013) who assume that "LMS have a limited functionality to support educational activities from a socio-constructive perspective" (p. 68). Similarly, the study by Dabbagh and Kitsantas (2011) reported that institutionally approved LMS do not allow informal learning to occur. According to Dabbagh and Kitsantas, in contrast with LMS, social media "can facilitate the creation of personal learning environments" that "support a learner-centered pedagogy and foster self-regulated learning" (p. 3).

Setting Course Rules and Expectations

Another important aspect that emerges is participants strong belief of a need for rules and expectations for course-related communications on social media. Aside from the occasional discussions with students about ethical challenges associated with interactivity on social media, participants recognize the importance of creating a "code of conduct" or "social rules". One participant went the extra mile, creating Tumblr exemplars to encourage students to adopt ethical social media practices.

We always did at the start of every new semester what we called an expectation session. It would really be about making students think about themselves in this learning environment, what are their expectations of the teaching staff and what are their expectations regarding the other learners... What we said is that nothing's gonna change when we go to online space. You want this collaborative supportive learning environment in the classroom. Do you want that online as well? This was our kind of structure-setting method. So our first tutorial or a laboratory session guided students through how to use Moodle, what is a Facebook site, what kind of things to expect in different places.

You have a variety of students with different capabilities and skills in terms of communication... Facebook allows raising opinions. It's important not to take it [comments/opinions] personally...Once you draw the line and say "This is what we do", then it makes a lot easier. Students start recognizing the value.

While participants point out differences in teaching, with the use of LMS and social media, in certain aspects these platforms are remarkably similar. There is a fundamental commonality that has everything to do with the institutional control over learning processes. Even on social media where acceptance for "supporting informal learning" (Garmendía & Cobos, 2013, p. 68) and "personal learning environments" (Dabbagh & Kitsantas, 2011) is growing, these participants seem to follow a highly formalized procedure of knowledge production and distribution.

Managing Course Information and Students Access to the Course Materials

A number of participants state that social media allows them to organize and manage course information more effectively. In this regard, participants generally emphasize 'simplicity', 'seamlessness', 'all-in-one' and 'easy-to-use' as the persistent qualities of social media that apply equally well to course information management, activities design and content distribution:

Lots of different resources can be stored e.g. links, photos, quotations, video links and chat.

It [course content] is all there and they [students] share with each other. So if someone is not there, then it doesn't matter.

It [social media] is also a sharing platform for the assessments – they can share documents, images and presentations.

An interesting point was made in regard to the possibility of quickly and easily modifying the course content when needed. It seems to be an important quality of social media as well, particularly when it comes to group work and class discussions:

Students can reblog and change a caption to a comment.

Whatever they have [sketches, notes on a piece of paper] – it goes to social media to a Facebook group. I asked them to record their presentations [at home], then to upload presentations on FB. I also asked students to provide constructive feedback on their classmates' work.

Most important to highlight in this context is that participants feel that, in contrast to Moodle, social media offers a more convenient way to make course information and any course-related activities and updates available to students in a timely fashion. The study shows that participants often use Facebook "as a forum to post information about the class and what was happening".

We know forums are pretty dead now, it's very difficult to get students use them. [Students) were not using Moodle forums, they weren't engaging with anything. All of the institutional emails went to their institutional student accounts that they never checked... Instead they were [on Facebook] on their phones...

Moodle isn't so user-friendly. You can have people hanging out there and having a conversation...

Having said that, the comparison of Moodle and social media, specifically Facebook, did not lead to an assumption that social media could replace the LMS. This is in contrast to Wang et al., (2012) who, as mentioned above, claimed that participants viewed social media as an adjunct to LMS.

I don't see how the course can be completely taught on social media yet. It's still a part of, not a whole.

If there is an assignment or slides – they go on Moodle.

There is an agreement between all participants that social media may best be used as a collaborative platform for group projects, course information updates, timely feedback, and after-class revision activities. For example, it was quite common among participants to use social media for debriefing topics covered in class by asking students clarifying questions. One participant mentioned that she uses Facebook for tutorials: *"I asked students questions and they responded"*. There is not enough evidence to suggest that social media had also been incorporated in the assessment practices, excluding formative. However, a number of participants have begun to develop summative assessments with social media components to enrich students' learning experiences within real world contexts.

Facilitating Group Collaboration

What has become evident during the data analysis is that participants agree that social media helps them facilitate group collaboration. More precisely, the participants believe that social media allows for better group work and collaborative learning. This takes can take different forms: from those that are strictly focused on group assignment completion to those that encourage follow up discussions and peer feedback.

All assessments are mainly group assessments...The final assessment is running the event, so it's a lot of intense group work. They [students] have a lot of documents and FB gives them the chance to post quick questions.

The data also reveals that participants believe that collaborative learning on social media resulted in students' "better judgments and personal reflection" and overall, students' active contributions to the group work:

I usually get students into groups based on their specializations (marketing, sales, finance). I ask them to work on different business ideas or on a particular project. Once they finish it, they are expected to present [their projects] to other groups...I believe that it's critical to have more conversations on the subject matter... it can help them [students] to move forward.

Participants also pointed out that social media is an effective instrument in encouraging self-regulated group work:

If [students] not contributing, this was obvious to group who could work out what to do instead of a lecturer having to intervene.

Realizing the advantages of social media, some participants are able to extend student group projects far beyond the Facebook closed groups, focusing on productive collaboration between students and relevant industry partners through various tasks and interactions on social media:

[My] papers are completely practical. The whole aim has been to create an event from scratch working as a team. We typically team up with an organization that runs an event...We create an event schedule – event postings under their name.

Another participant strongly believes that assessments that incorporate social media, either for group projects or students' self-directed learning, support a smoother transition from the classroom to industry for students:

I want to produce employable students...we are going to be proactive, on top of the game. My assignments are based on real companies. Many of them have FB page. What you do? You like the page, see what the company is doing, their latest tweets or the latest updates on their FB page. As a lecturer you can say "hey, your assignment is based on that company, go and check their page". And they start getting feeds from it...Being connected to the industry online, they learn the language they speak.

At this stage, it is important to note that participants often refer to students' careers and employability as the primary drivers behind activities designed for social media:

We want to teach students how to build their personal brands on social media. People have their own brands now and they don't stay with one company forever.

A social media presence can be important. A lot of companies now do look at social media...So there is a responsibility students need to realize – what they put on Facebook may be available to people. It makes them more employable.

This result is supported by McLoughlin and Lee's study (2010) that highlighted an educational need to move towards "a social and participatory pedagogy" that supports students "personal life goals" in the changing job markets where "individuals are expected to have multiple career paths..." (p. 31).

In concluding these findings on social media as a course management tool, it is important to note that, despite the positive experiences presented above, the adaptation of social media as a course design and delivery tool is not straightforward. One research participant raises some doubts as to what extent a teacher should be involved in online learning spaces such as Facebook closed groups:

I'm not a part of students' conversation...I'm not in the groups. I have been in a previous class. I was worried that they are aware I was watching. So it can stop some of the process. This time around I have decided not to be a part of the groups...I do check how the group is going. Who is sitting on social media but not coming to class. Are they active?

This example indicates something particularly interesting about the current stage of social media use in education. On the one hand, understanding the advantages of social media, the participants intensively used it for group projects and students' independent study, or even for supporting students' "transition from classroom to the industry". On the other hand, in many cases the course groups on social media were created, owned and controlled by research participants. This means that course materials, the way they were presented and distributed to students, course discussions, content and activities had been decided and developed by teachers. From the institutional point of view this is not surprising, as social media is still a new and challenging learning space for education. Moreover, teachers and learning designers are greatly limited by specific institutional policies and arrangements within which social media can be adapted and applied to the course design. The result is somewhat consistent with the findings of Hemmi, Bayne, and Landt (2009) on social technologies in higher education: "we found a tendency for both teachers and learners to 'rein in' these potential radical and challenging effects of the new media formations, to control and constrain them within more orthodox understanding of ...formal learning" (p. 29).

Even though the research participants welcome social media as "a new learning space" that "gives students some room" to have control over the course, managing and regulating students' learning were still strong priorities for participants.

Theme 2: Student-Centered Teaching Practices

The second key theme to emerge from this study is the use of social media to enhance student-centered teaching practices. Student-centered teaching refers to teaching practices that are responsive to students' individual and group learning needs. Educators using these practices take on the role of assistant to the student's learning, encourage students to become active, independent participants in the learning process, and use knowledge as a tool rather than a goal of learning (Baeten, Kyndt, Struyven & Dochy, 2010).

Research on social media in education often mentions collaboration, community building, creation of new content and forming personal identities as uses of social media in education (Tess, 2013). However, there is little mention of the use of social media as a tool for student-centered learning and teaching. At least some features of student-centered learning are mentioned by all participants in this research and one lecturer in particular specifically explores a student-centered learning pedagogy in her use of social media.

Using Social Media to Understand Students' Background and Knowledge

In order to be able to support and respond to individual students' learning needs, participants in this research use social media to learn about and better understand their students' background, skills and knowledge. All the participants report that social media platforms appear to make information on student skills and knowledge more accessible.

You know a lot about your students through Facebook. What skills they could bring in. Are they weak at English or they are weak at the subject? And based on that you help them. It makes it so easy for learning to occur.

[Social media is] familiar so it automatically makes them feel comfortable. [Social media] shows other student capabilities. Start with what the student knows and respect that. Using a variety of media to capture students and their world tapped into more skills.

[Social media allows] to know your learner, what commitments they have. I had a student... Through connecting with him on FB I realized he was a

young parent with young kids and he actually needed a bit more support. What they see is support – the teacher can help me out if I need it.

An idea was... what is their prior knowledge coming to the session.

Using Social Media to Support Students and Encourage Independence

The participants' interest extends beyond just knowing their students. This knowledge of students' strengths and requirements allows the lecturers to support, scaffold and guide the students' learning more effectively. These lecturers also wanted to build on the students' prior understanding and to encourage students to use their own knowledge and worldviews in their learning. These actions both increase students' confidence and independence and their understanding of knowledge as a tool, important aspects of student-centered learning (Baeten et al, 2010).

It is student-centered; it is co-constructivist. Students build their own efficacy and knowledge. [The learning is] student directed and the lecturer scaffolds.

I would ask them to start with "What is the best way for you to communicate?"

We are facilitators we don't know everything.

Students can bring more of their world. Students as the center of their knowledge. Build own efficacy and knowledge, start with what student knows and respect that.

If someone wasn't contributing [on the social media site] this was obvious to group who could work out what to do instead of lecturer having to intervene.

[Students] ease with it and so it makes students more confident increases learning especially less academic students.

Lecturers as Assistants to Learners and Learning

Using social media enables lecturers to access students' work as it progresses, often in real time. This means lecturers are able to provide not only more immediate feedback and support, but also make interventions that are focused on individual need. Rather than supplying more general teacher-led directions, lecturers can assist with individual students' learning needs and highlight students' questions and concerns. This support encourages more active independent learning, further enhancing student-centered learning.

The last 5-10 minutes we quickly scrolled through that FB page and noticed some questions that came up more than few times - do we want to explore more? This kind of use is really powerful. Instant feedback you probably wouldn't get out elsewhere.

[You can] keep an eye on progress and you can support immediately. I displayed files on board as shared and this spurred students to complete and share documents. Instant feedback.

[Social media allows] being reactive to their [students] needs.

They can challenge me .. it can help them to move forward.

Culturally Inclusive

Key student-centered learning for one of the participants in this research means ensuring a safe cultural space where students can express their own knowledge, cultural identity and background. In a bicultural tertiary context, this place for cultural identity is essential (Ministry of Education, n.d). Creating a bicultural environment may allow those who feel outside the norm to find a place for self-expression, countering the predominantly western cultural framework of social media platforms. The lecturer below references the NZ Early Childhood Curriculum document, Te Whariki, as her students are Early Childhood pathway students. In this curriculum particular emphasis is placed on bicultural and inclusive practice (Ministry of Education, 1996).

I wanted a way students could be themselves and bring whanau, traditional knowing etc., and bring this to their work...I wanted the course to privilege their knowledge...Students in center of their knowledge, experts in own cultures.

Much research into the use of social media in learning and teaching centers around social collaboration. This data suggests that, as well as collaboration, using social media platforms facilitates lecturers to incorporate student-centered teaching practice into their courses. For participants in this research, social media allows better access to understanding their students' skills and learning needs. This knowledge of the students helps the lecturers to respond and scaffold student learning in a more individual and focused way and in a more timely manner, thus encouraging students to become more independent learners. In addition, allowing students a place in the class to bring their own knowledge and identity, particularly cultural identity, further increases students' confidence and encourages independent learning and use of their prior knowledge as a resource. By using social media in their courses, lecturers are assisting rather than directing student learning, encouraging independent learning and applying rather than accumulating knowledge. All these aspects give a strong sense of student-centered practice in the research participants' social media-based teaching practice and suggests an interesting avenue for further research.

Theme 3: Institutional Support

Social media platforms provide tools that can support good teaching practice by improving student- teacher interactions (Tess, 2013). As with any new tool, lecturers need guidance with best practice, ongoing discussions with colleagues and access to communities of practice. These are aspects of the social resources provided by the community, society and institutions that support and enable implementation of any new technologies (Warschauer, 2003). Without these social resources, particularly institutional support, implementation of new technology is impeded (Warschauer, 2003).

In addition, the use of commercial platforms adds some ethical and safety risks for students, staff and the institution. Commercial social media sites are developed and promoted for commercial gain, and access to these sites typically requires users to agree that their individual data will be collected and sold. It is usually not possible to opt out of these conditions (Fuchs, 2014). Social media sites are also designed to allow open access and the significance of this to students' safety needs to be considered both by lecturers and institutions.

A significant theme identified by the participants in this research centers around the lack of institutional support. Both social resources and institutional management of ethical and safety risks are highlighted by the participants as a concern in their implementation of social media in their courses.

Support for Teaching Practice

While participants use social media platforms as part of good teaching practice, they feel that the institute and senior staff provide little support and sometimes actively discourage their use of social media. Although blended and online learning are embedded in the institute's learning and teaching, participants' report that their use of social media does not seem to be accepted as an aspect of this type of learning. Lack of support from senior staff and academic advisors leads many participants to keep their use of social media to themselves and a few supportive colleagues. In comparison with other online tools, participants' use of social media appears to be less acceptable as a valid learning and teaching tool. In particular, participants mention lack of advice from experienced lecturers and little access to best practice teaching resources.

The decision was made between my colleague and myself. We were mavericks. The department had quite an old school type senior staff. So our attitude was let's just do it and see how it works. And then talk to senior staff about what we have done because they would get a lot of barriers we were already working through from the staff.

I wasn't sure if I should be doing that. Some people from [our academic advisory team] thought it was a bad idea, so I kept it low. But I thought the students are there, the concepts are there. I'm very confident about it

No training [in using social media]

A lot of the time with new staff we just kind of muddling along with what works for now. Eventually we make it official, and put a structure around. But it's definitely better to have more advice.

We didn't have any real infrastructure [for using social media].

Safety Issues

As Tess (2013) notes, the choice to use social media often comes from the educators rather than the institution and this certainly seems to be the case for the educators in this research. However, social media platforms, and particularly commercial social media platforms, are not without risks. Most staff institute some measures to increase students' safety: closed groups; instructions about the safety features of platforms; and how to communicate online. Although probably rare events, both trolling and stalking can and do occur on social media platforms and, as some authors have noted, use of social media can have deleterious effects (Lin et al, 2016; Tess 2013). Not all staff seem to recognize these safety issues.

For me privacy settings are much better on Instagram. I have stopped posting pictures of my son on Facebook. I now use Instagram as a very private account and only accepted close family.

You have access to personal accounts of students and see things about them. Whilst I'm not interested that's what I can see. I don't think that's appropriate for them or for me.

The biggest question was always around the privacy of the students and how we can maintain a closed network.

And a lot of people didn't understand social media, how it works, can we really engage on social media, so their questions were the same as most people who are very resistant. What does it mean to the students, how can they be safe in this space?

[Tumblr] feels safer, no nasty comments and can't get trolled or be stalked. I've had mine public and never had any problems.

Ethical Issues

Not unexpectedly, most participants use commercial social media platforms themselves and appear to choose these platforms in their teaching. As the top ten most popular social media platforms (Chaffey, 2017) are commercial businesses, the likelihood, as for participants in this research, is that lecturers and designers choose to use commercial social media platforms. The priority of these platforms is to collect and sell data to other businesses. This raises issues around student awareness of this collection and sale of their data and the ethics, for educators and tertiary institutions, colluding in this practice. Although some concerns are expressed for online safety, most participants do not seem to consider exposing students to data collection by third parties as an issue for their students, themselves or their institution.

Having data collected is part and parcel of using social media – it's a free platform.

Who stores the data...so we tried to stay away from that and really used it as a tool for engagement and another space for students' learning, not assessing.

Not all students are comfortable engaging with social media platforms (Salmon, Ross, Pechenkina, & Chase, 2015). Furthermore, some consideration must be taken into the power relationship between lecturers and their students. Although none of these lecturers insist that students sign up to social media platforms, the power relationship between lecturer and student can coerce students into joining social media platforms that their lecturer seems to endorse. Students may assume that the lecturer requires the use of a particular social media platform or that not using that platform could affect their grade for the course.

We had one or two students throughout the course of 3 years who said, "we don't like FB, we don't want to use it". With those students what we did – we sat down and explain why we're using social media, what the purpose was and they actually said they felt they see value in what we try to do. And it was only one student ever who didn't sign up for an account. What we did for these students, we emailed them with information we give everyone else.

One student told me that he is not so keen on using the Internet, he is kind of old school. And I asked him that what he wanted to do future wise. And I said 'To be honest, you need to get on with that because today if you want to be successful you need to have the understanding at least of how we use these things.

[You] shouldn't make anyone who refuses. You can't make them and neither should you.

I don't think anyone's told us any guidelines around it [social media] and that's shocking.

Policies for using social media platforms in learning and teaching, a code of conduct, and ethics for staff and students are essential for the safety of students, staff and tertiary institution. However, policies which might cover the use of social media in these tertiary institutions are myriad and often contradictory (Willems, Adachi, & Grevtseva, 2016). Although lecturers in this study are generally not concerned with these issues, this may be because at present the use of social media in their teaching is limited. Social media platforms "serve interests and priorities other than (and in many cases opposed to) those of learning" (Friesen and Lowe, 2011, p. 11). With this in mind, tertiary institutions have a duty of care to staff and students to plan for the safe and ethical use of social media in tertiary education.

SOLUTIONS AND RECOMMENDATIONS

As discussed earlier, social media is changing the way learning is designed and delivered to students. The integration of social media in course content areas, resources, activities and assessment practices is expected to continue. This study acknowledges that social media is not the only avenue for tertiary education, but rather a supporting tool for some aspects of course management and student-centered teaching practices. Based on key themes presented in this study, the following solutions and recommendations can be put forward:

1. There is a need to create and test what Dalsgaard (2006) calls "social software" that can "move e-learning beyond learning management systems and engage students in an active use of the web as a resource for their self-governed, problem-based and collaborative activities". According to study participants, existing learning management systems do not perform well in the context of collaborative learning and cannot be considered as a stand-alone platform for delivering education.
2. The findings of this study suggest that in order to effectively use social media in teaching, educators need to recognize students' pre-existing experiences, knowledge and skills. This approach suggests that teachers should incorporate this information into the course curriculum and teaching and involve students in course design. This could allow designing and delivering courses in ways that encourage "participation, community connections, social interaction and global networking" (McLoughlin, & Lee, 2010, p. 38).

3.   The findings also reveal that a broad-scale discussion about ethical and legal issues around social media is needed "in order to guide faculty members and administrators through the decision related to social media use" (Cain & Fink, 2010, p. 7). The integration of social media in learning and teaching also requires a systematic approach to professional and constructive dialog with students.

FUTURE RESEARCH DIRECTIONS

As with many new educational tools, social media is being implemented into learning and teaching, while research into these practices lags behind. In addition, the emerging research into social media in education often focuses on issues of collaborative learning, communities of practice and creation of content, possibly reflecting the perceived personal uses of social media. The research in this chapter highlights some different uses of social media in tertiary education showing that, in practice, learning designers and lecturers find social media platforms beneficial as learning management tools and in increasing student-centered learning practices. Further research is needed to explore these aspects of social media in education.

These research findings also suggest that social media may be useful in supporting other teaching practices outside the previously mentioned social and content generation aspects. This research shows how educators are already engaged in using social media in interesting and different ways in their teaching, so that researching these practices is not only essential but urgent. Action-based research into current practices would provide a means to engage with this current use of social media in education.

Future research into teaching practice of course relies on the support of educational institutions. As is seen in this chapter, educational institutions can be ambivalent towards the use of social media in education. For further research to occur, educational institutes need to accept that their lecturers will continue to use social media in their teaching and should therefore support the investigations needed to increase the understanding of the best practice use of social media in education.

CONCLUSION

The use of social media in tertiary institutes has grown as social media use has expanded into everyday life. These platforms were not created for education purposes but were developed to be easily accessible and simple to use. Driven by commercial gains, social media companies will continue to develop intuitive, easy to use and engaging platforms drawing in both students and educators as users. In contrast, online education learning management systems were designed, initially at least, as a repository for resources and for the use of educators not students. Although LMS have become more interactive, students are now more familiar using social media sites to connect and post content and appear more engaged with social media platforms.

It is not only the ease of use that drives educators to social media sites. Lecturers recognize significant benefits to using social media in both greater efficiency of learning management and increased student involvement in their learning. These advantages are tempered by educators' concerns with the support that educational institutions provide with resources, best practice and minimization of risk, issues that need to be addressed if the full advantages of using social media in learning and teaching can be realized.

In conclusion the authors hope this research will inspire further development of new teaching practices into the use of social media in tertiary education and further research that will inform these practices.

REFERENCES

Bosch, T. E. (2009). Using online social networking for teaching and learning: Facebook use at the University of Cape Town. *Communication, 35*(2), 185–200.

Cain, J., & Fink, J. L. III. (2010). Legal and ethical issues regarding social media and Pharmacy education. *American Journal of Pharmaceutical Education, 74*(10), 1–8. doi:10.5688/aj7410184 PMID:21436925

Chaffey, D. (2017). *Global social media research summary 2017*. Retrieved from http://www.smartinsights.com/social-media-marketing/social-media-strategy/new-global-social-media-research/

Corbin, J., & Strauss, A. (2015). *Basics of qualitative research: Techniques and procedures for developing grounded theory* (4th ed.). Thousand Oaks, CA: SAGE.

Dabbagh, N., & Kitsantas, A. (2011). Personal Learning Environments, social media, and self-regulated learning: A natural formula for connecting formal and informal learning. *Internet and Higher Education., 15*(1), 3–8. doi:10.1016/j.iheduc.2011.06.002

Dalsgaard, C. (2006). Social software: E-learning beyond learning management systems. *European Journal of Open, Distance and E-Learning, 2006*(2). Retrieved from http://www.eurodl.org/index.php?p=archives&year=2006 &hal&article=228

Friesen, N., & Lowe, S. (2012). The questionable promise of social media for education: Connective learning and the commercial imperative. *Journal of Computer Assisted Learning, 28*(3), 183–194. doi:10.1111/j.1365-2729.2011.00426.x

Fuchs, C. (2014). *Social media: A critical introduction.* London: Sage. doi:10.4135/9781446270066.n2

Garmendía, A., & Cobos, R. (2013). Towards the extension of a LMS with social media services. In *Proceedings of the 10th International Conference on Cooperative Design, Visualization, and Engineering.* Berlin: Springer. 10.1007/978-3-642-40840-3_11

Griesemer, A. (2012). Using social media to enhance students' learning experiences. *Quality Approaches in Higher Education, 3*(1), 8–11.

Hemmi, A., Bayne, S., & Landt, R. (2009). The appropriation and repurposing of social technologies in higher education. *Journal of Computer Assisted Learning, 25*(1), 19–30. doi:10.1111/j.1365-2729.2008.00306.x

Hootsuite. (2017). *Social campus report: A global survey of higher education social media usage.* Retrieved from https://hootsuite.com/resources/social-campus-report#

Kofinas, A. K., Al-Shawakbeh, A., & Lim, A. S. (2016). Key success factors of using social media as a learning tool. In V. Benson, R. Tuninga, & G. Saridakis (Eds.), *Analyzing the strategic role of social networking in firms growth and productivity.* IGI Global; doi:10.4018/978-1-5225-0559-4

Lin, L. Y., Sidani, J. E., Shensa, A., Radovic, A., Miller, E., Colditz, J. B., ... Primack, B. A. (2016). Association between social media use and depression among U.S. young adults. *Depression and Anxiety, 33*(4), 323–331. doi:10.1002/da.22466 PMID:26783723

McLoughlin, C., & Lee, M. J. W. (2010). Personalised and self-regulated learning in the Web 2.0 era: International exemplars of innovative pedagogy using social software. *Australasian Journal of Educational Technology*, *26*(1), 28–43. doi:10.14742/ajet.1100

Ministry of Education. (1996). *Te Whariki*. Wellington: Learning Media Limited. Retrieved from https://www.education.govt.nz/assets/Documents/Early-Childhood/te-whariki.pdf

Ministry of Education. (n.d.). *Frameworks for bicultural education – He anga mō te mātauranga ahurea rua*. Retrieved from https://www.education.govt.nz/early-childhood/teaching-and-learning/assessment-for-learning/kei-tua-o-te-pae-2/bicultural-assessment-he-aromatawai-ahurea-rua/frameworks-for-bicultural-education-he-anga-mo-te-matauranga-ahurea-rua/

Piven, I., & Breazeale, M. (2016). Desperately seeking customer engagement: The five-sources model of brand value on social media. In V. Benson, R. Tuninga, & G. Saridakis (Eds.), *Analyzing strategic role of social networking in firms growth and productivity*. IGI Global; doi:10.4018/978-1-5225-0559-4

Roblyer, M. D., McDaniel, M., Webb, M., Herman, J., & Witty, J. V. (2010). Findings on Facebook in higher education: A comparison of college faculty and student uses and perceptions of social networking sites. *Internet and Higher Education*, *13*(3), 134–140. doi:10.1016/j.iheduc.2010.03.002

Salmon, G., Ross, B., Pechenkina, E., & Chase, A. (2015). The space for social media in structured online learning. *Research in Learning Technology*, *23*(1), 28507. doi:10.3402/rlt.v23.28507

Samovar, L. A., & Porter, R. E. (2003). *Intercultural communication: A reader* (10th ed.). Belmont: Thomson Learning.

Tess, P. (2013). The role of social media in higher education classes (real and virtual): A literature review. *Computers in Human Behavior*, *29*(5), A60–A68. doi:10.1016/j.chb.2012.12.032

Wang, Q., Woo, H. L., Quek, C. L., Yang, Y., & Liu, M. (2012). Using the Facebook group as a learning management system: An exploratory study. *British Journal of Educational Technology*, *43*(3), 428–438. doi:10.1111/j.1467-8535.2011.01195.x

Willems, J., Adachi, C., & Grevtseva, Y. (2016, January). Working with social media in tertiary education: A contested space between academics and policies. In ASCILITE Adelaide 2016: Show Me the Learning (pp. 648-653). Australasian Society for Computers in Learning in Tertiary Education.

ADDITIONAL READING

Benson, V. (2014). *Cutting-edge technologies and social media use in higher education*. IGI Global. doi:10.4018/978-1-4666-5174-6

Bicen, H., & Uzunboylu, H. (2013). The use of social networking sites in education: A case study of Facebook. *Journal of Universal Computer Science*, *19*(5), 658–671.

Carpenter, J. P. (2014). Twitter's capacity to support collaborative learning. *International Journal of Social Media and Interactive Learning Environments*, *2*(2), 103–118. doi:10.1504/IJSMILE.2014.063384

Ha, J., & Shin, D. H. (2014). Facebook in a standard college class: An alternative conduit for promoting teacher-student interaction. *American Communication Journal*, *16*(1), 36–52.

Manca, S., & Ranieri, M. (2016). Yes for sharing, no for teaching!: Social media in academic practices. *The Internet and Higher Education*, *29*, 63–74. doi:10.1016/j.iheduc.2015.12.004

Pitrick, R. M., & Holzinger, A. (2002). Student-centered teaching meets new media: Concept and case study. *Journal of Educational Technology & Society*, *5*(4), 160–172.

Rodrigue, J. E. (2011). Social media use in higher education: Key areas to consider for educators. *MERLOT. Journal of Online Learning and Teaching / MERLOT*, *7*(4), 539–550.

Voorn, R. J. J., & Kommers, P. A. M. (2013). Social media and higher education: Introversion and collaborative learning from the student's perspective. *International Journal of Social Media and Interactive Learning Environments*, *1*(1), 59–73. doi:10.1504/IJSMILE.2013.051650

KEY TERMS AND DEFINITIONS

Collaborative Learning: Groups of students work together to complete a task which is designed to enhance teamwork, knowledge sharing and building, and learning from each other.

Course Management: Course management is the process of creating, implementing, and coordinating the learning and teaching activities in order to achieve the course specification and defined learning outcomes.

Institutional Support: As part of the social resources required to assist implementation of new (educational) practices, this support consists of the resources an organization provides including financial, policies, and guidelines.

Learning and Teaching: Educational practices that students and teachers engage in to promote acquisition and application of knowledge.

Learning Design: The teaching-learning process of enhancing students' learning experiences by creating relevant course content areas, resources, activities, and assessments.

Learning Management System: A digital "all-in-one" course management application that organizes course activities and resources, and delivers administrative functions for the course.

Student-Centered Teaching: An educational practice whereby students, as the focus of the learning and teaching, are supported by teachers to become independent learners.

Tertiary Education: Learning in an educational institute that occurs post-secondary school. This may be academic or vocational learning.

Tumblr: A microblogging service that incorporates elements of social media as users can follow each other, "like" each others' content, and/ or "reblog" content posted by other users. The platform allows users to post a variety of content including images, text, videos, links, and audio.

Chapter 6
Future Directions:
Emergent Social Media Technologies and the Potential for Higher Education

Ann M. Simpson
Unitec Institute of Technology, New Zealand

ABSTRACT

This chapter considers future directions for emerging social media technologies and their potential for teaching and learning practice in higher education. While technologies that support social media constantly change, it provides some simple and practical guidelines to assist teachers with their practice and use of social media technologies in their classrooms. This chapter acknowledges the evolving nature of the technologies available in today's teaching and learning context as well as ones that are considered to impact higher educational learning and teaching in the future, including descriptions of augmented and virtual reality and gamification and gamified learning.

INTRODUCTION

Technology has always brought change to society. New electronic tools and activities that social media and educational technologies facilitate seem to offer promise with tremendous potential to transform educational environments (Veletsianos, 2010). However, a solid definition of emergent technologies is difficult to define and is as nebulous and ever-changing as the technologies seem to be. What exactly are emergent technologies and what are the potentials of these technologies in higher education? How can emergent

DOI: 10.4018/978-1-5225-5826-2.ch006

social media technologies be defined, if in a continued state of change? What about technologies that seem to embed social media elements such as live, online chats and forums, commonly referred to as social media affordances? Veletsianos describes emergent technologies in terms of its 'importance of impact' (Veletsianos, 2010). 'Importance of impact' is viewed as 'leading edge' because it is unknown and seems to have an edge of possibility that has not yet been investigated (Veletsianos, 2010).

However, social media is more often defined through example (Tess, 2013). We know what the technologies are or when they appear in our classrooms with students, however, how can we define emergent in the educational context? While social media has not traditionally been designed for educational contexts, what are the current social media technologies and technologies with social media affordances that can potentially throw light onto the future potential of social media use in higher education? While it is impossible to predict the future, we can attempt to contextualize emerging technologies and the potential of those technologies as possible indicators for future social media trends (Parsons, 2014). This chapter considers the emergent state of social media and social media affordances present in emergent technologies and considers possible future directions and potential in higher education.

BACKGROUND

Worldwide use of social media will continue to grow (Chaffey, 2017). Based on the sheer numbers of active users of social media for business and personal use is approximately 24% of the world's population; growth will continue globally with great potential for use in tertiary settings (Chaffey, 2017; United Nations, 2017). While the digital divide remains an issue, access to the support technologies and infrastructure can be facilitated by governmental programs (Adams Becker, Cumins, et al., 2017, 2017; Unesco, 2016). Underlying infrastructures, technologies and affordances of devices will continue to change creating potential opportunities. A greater number of programs and applications are offering the affordances of Web 2.0 technologies enabling some form of social interaction, e.g. the ability to conduct live chats while editing in a Google Doc. Moreover, augmented reality, virtual reality and gamified learning offer even more social media alternatives and potential for the higher education classroom. The lines are becoming blurred as to where the social meets the media's purpose; i.e. social tools, such as chats and forums, can be found in virtually any program or application.

Technologies have surrounded educational contexts since the advent of the computer. The technologies offer increasing options for blended learning environments. Reports regarding the trends and possibilities of emergent technologies such as The NMC New Horizons report and the ECAR Study of Undergraduate Students and Information Technology, and the JISC student digital experience tracker report, released yearly and are highly anticipated as they provide valuable information about upcoming trends and technology developments in higher education (Adams Becker, Cumins, et al., 2017; Adams Becker, Cummins, et al., 2017; Brooks, 2016; Newman & Beetham, 2017; Veletsianos, 2016). The NMC New Horizons and ECAR reports attempt to anticipate future trends based on potential impact to higher education. The demand for information about future directions is important for institutions in terms of strategic planning and implementation of technologies that will suit their digital and academic strategies. However, as emergent technologies and changing contexts have altered to become more modular and mobile, the nature of emergent social media technologies has impacted the higher education environment in unique ways. Learning has become more contextual, personal, and evolved to placing learning in any location (Parsons, 2014).

EMERGING TECHNOLOGIES AND PRACTICE

Veletsianos in the book Emerging Technologies in Distance Education defined emergent technologies as "tools, concepts, innovations, advancements, and practices" and that such technologies are dependent upon a variety of contexts (Veletsianos, 2016, p. 4). Veletsianos highlights the fact that technologies may not be brand new, meaning new to market technologies, but are more likely to be pre-existing technologies utilized in new contexts. For example, Veletsianos cited the use of electronic whiteboards use in the UK, and while they were highly utilized in English primary schools, uptake and use of them in higher educational contexts proved more difficult (Veletsianos, 2010). Veletsianos also acknowledged that new technologies exist in a stage of coming into being surrounded by an unknown factor, sometimes wrapped in media hype (Veletsianos, 2010). Emergent technologies are not fully understood nor are they fully researched; they are not always utilized to their full extent because they are in fact, evolving and being released and re-released to their target audiences and markets (Veletsianos, 2010). For example, new versions of android smart phones or iPhones are released to consumers on a yearly basis. However, in in a later article, The Defining Characteristics of Emerging Technologies and Emerging Practices in Digital Education, Veletsianos further honed the definition by separating out <u>practice</u> of the emergent technologies from the <u>use</u> of them (Veletsianos, 2016). That is, how the technologies were designed to be used versus how they are actually used. Veletsianos continued to describe the emergent practice of those technologies as unique and discipline specific (Veletsianos, 2016). In the case of social media technologies, the programs and applications are becoming more and more discipline specific, for example Sermo is the largest social media networking website for doctors in the world or ResearchGate or Academia.edu the two largest social networking sites for academics (Manca & Ranieri, 2016; Palmer & Strickland, 2017; Reisenwitz, 2017). While the technologies constantly change, so too are the practices and use of those emergent technologies by the audiences who choose to utilize them. Emergent technologies will continue to exist and will continue to have an aura of 'unknown' or mystery about them. However, the emergent practice occurs when others share and <u>use</u> those suggested practices in their own practice, communities, and learning networks. This chapter uses Veltsianos' description of the practice and use of emergent technologies in the social media context as a starting point to consider potential possibilities and directions of social media technologies and affordances for higher education.

CONTEXTS FOR THE EMERGENT ENVIRONMENT

It is important to consider the context for the emerging environment in which the social media tools will be present. The evolution of the "bring your own device" movement in the workplaces has extended into higher education (Afreen, 2014). Along with these new mobile technologies arrived software programs and applications that utilized the affordances of the devices themselves such as cameras and microphones. Many of these devices arrive with their own software programs and applications installed on them to leverage these tools, for example, voice recognition software for the Google search engine. In addition, due to the mobility of these technologies, the devices and software contained in them could be used in any location. Personalized, context specific mobile use of the devices became more feasible for individuals and social media became mobile social media, thus extending the possible contexts through the Bring Your Own Device movement, mobile social media, and personalization.

BYO: What?

In 2009, Intel Corporation recognized that employees wanted to bring their own devices in the workplace. In recognition of this, the corporation instituted the world's first Bring Your Own Device policy (BYOD) (Roman, 2011). Today, in higher educational institutions, it is common-place for students to connect their own devices to their institutional networks due to BYOD policies (Siddiqui, 2014). Alongside the BYOD policies and required networking environments, the software installed on the devices should be considered along with institutional BYOD and recommended software policies (Siddiqui, 2014; Van Leeuwen, 2014). With the proliferation of 'free' social media software applications such as YouTube, Twitter, and Facebook, many instructors and students choose to use these software packages instead evolving into a Bring Your Own Software (BYOS) environment (Chaffey, 2017; Hootsuite Media, Inc, 2017; Van Leeuwen, 2014). Van Leeuwen suggests reasons for this include: ease of use for the chosen software, the software's compatibility with devices, and that often the software contains features that other programs lack (2014). In addition, it is responsibility of the software company not the institution, instructors, or students to upgrade the software providing additional benefit. However, Helman continues the Bring Your Own continuum and argues that the higher education environment has evolved into a Bring Your Own Everything (BYOE) environment (2014). Students customize and use their devices and software for personal use and safety aided by the Wi-Fi connectivity to everyday things from door locks to exercise equipment (Helman, 2014). Privacy issues will continue as students use with their devices and software, knowingly or unknowingly (DeMers, 2017; Jacobsson, 2010).

As the numbers of social media users in higher education continue to rise, the opportunities for social media use through BYOD and BYOS software policies in the higher education classroom will continue to increase (Hootsuite Media, Inc, 2017; Siddiqui, 2014; Van Leeuwen, 2014). New devices and mainly the software on them can provide additional opportunities to engage learners. Nevertheless, it will be up to the institutions to make decisions in terms of privacy and use of social media tools. How does this impact teaching and learning practice? Dependent upon use policies of the institution, teachers can choose to bring their own social media tools to the class to use – but perhaps consideration of digital citizenship, and rules of the road can be mutually agreed to at the classroom level first to insure student comfort and safety of their digital identity and data regardless of the social media tools and affordances utilized.

Mobile Social Media and Personalization

Mobile social media is social media that can be used on mobile devices. The nature of programs and applications developed for mobile social media are constantly being updated and improved and this change looks to continue in the future. While many software programs are created solely as social media applications, for example Facebook and Twitter, other software programs have developed to include social media affordances as they evolved. For example, YouTube offers the ability to post comments on video content in a forum format; the user community can view the comments about the video content and contribute to the discussion. In addition, users on YouTube can send private messages directly to the individuals that post the content. In the multi-player version of the online game, Minecraft, players can post "in-the-moment" comments live to the other players while simultaneously playing against each other in virtual worlds. While it is not this is not the sole purpose of the game this feature enables viewers and users to comment and participate in the conversations engendered by the media. Even word processing programs such as MS Word in Office 365 and Google Docs now also offer social media tools along contained within them, for example live chat and comments features.

Many of these programs and applications are mobile and provided an internet connection is available, users can access, interact, play, and engage in social media activities on the go regardless of location and time. The mobility of the devices combined with these social media affordances can create new possibilities for contextualized learning opportunities previously unavailable. The affordances now available in social media software and applications, allows students a large degree of personalization giving students more flexibility on how and when they choose to engage in their learning. Students can communicate these choices if they are allowed the opportunities to use social media tools in the classroom. A potential strategy could be for the instructor to discuss with students which social tools to use in class activities. The instructor can then insure co-creation and co-collaboration opportunities are present, that opportunities and activities are pedagogically informed and that the opportunities and activities are grounded in authentic, life-like contexts.

SOCIAL MEDIA PRACTICE: SUGGESTED GUIDELINES

While a significant body of research about the practices and contexts for the use of social media in many higher education disciplines exists, for the purposes of this chapter, a few suggested guidelines are proposed to assist in the selection of social media activities or tools for practice are considered and expanded upon (Manca & Ranieri, 2016; Veletsianos, 2010). Considerations about social media practice should include the following:

1. Social media practice is informed by pedagogy or learning purpose.
2. Social media practice allows for co-creative, co-collaborative learning opportunities.
3. Social media practice is informed by authentic, real life contexts.

While participation in a social media application could be as simple as 'liking' a post on a Facebook page, or 'liking' a live Ted Ex broadcast, they are social media activities representative of the individual user's context. As long as the activities are designed with underlying pedagogical principles in mind, they are considered educational social media activities (Parsons, 2014; Veletsianos, 2016). Once the technologies find their way into classes their use is molded by the "pedagogy and the educational practices and activities" (Veletsianos, 2016, p. 21). There must be some alignment with course objectives and learning outcomes, that is alignment with contextual, purposeful and meaningful social media opportunities and activity for students.

Co-creative and co-collaborative learning can be inherent in the social media technologies. A teacher requiring her students to participate in social media applications and activities continues to formulate a top down approach for its use. Whereas in its truest social collaborative form, the social media tools in fact are meant be utilized by the students and for the students in an educational context. This approach is leaving the opportunities open for students to choose their tools, activities and applications for the social media tools.

Finally, as pervasive as social media use is worldwide, students will, at some point have experience with the applications in a personal or professional capacity. Time spent on site utilizing tools in the real-world context are much more relevant to students and have potential to increase employability for them (Callan, Johnston, & Poulsen, 2015; Nore, 2015). These generic guidelines can assist in determining the suitability of the use of the emergent social media technologies and their potential in the classroom. Emerging technologies and practices transcend disciplines yet the different disciplines determine how they uptake and use those technologies (Manca & Ranieri, 2016). The social affordances utilized varies based on the purpose and needs of the discipline and social nature of the technologies leveraged. Uses of such technologies can be as individual and unique as the instructors who conduct the courses. An understanding of emergent practice guidelines can assist with laying the foundations for instructors to build their social media practices upon, while at the same time remaining open enough to allow instructors to determine flexibility and suitability for specific disciplines.

NOTABLE EMERGENT TECHNOLOGIES

The following technologies have been identified as possibly providing significant impact on social interaction, co-collaborative and co-creative applications in educational technology use. Many of these technologies either offer or will be able to offer social media affordances. These emergent technologies include the Internet of Things, augmented and virtual reality, and gamification and gamified learning.

Internet of Things

While digital contexts have the potential to change learning and teaching, the future of Web 3.0 technologies, the Internet of Things, sometimes called the semantic web, may also create educational change (Hew & Cheung, 2013). The internet of Things (IOT) is a word used to describe the micro devices which connect and share information to the internet other than smartphones, tablets and computers (Meola, 2016); that is, the IOT makes everyday items connectable to other devices and to the internet (Brown, 2017). An excellent example is the Fit Bit, a wearable technology that people to use monitor their physical activity including running, walking, biking, swimming, or sleeping.

The Internet of Things enables connectivity of the things you use in your daily life that can communicate with each other. This information is shared if the underlying technologies communicate with each other, and monitor,

Table 1. Internet of Things vignette: The case of the late student

The following is a vignette describes a possible scenario with and without the IOT:
Without the Internet of Things
Susan missed the alarm on her phone and woke up late for university because it was so cold and dark outside. She got up, rushed to get dressed, kicked the chair at the dining room table and bruised her knees as she ran out of the house, while neglecting to notice her cat needed to be fed. She missed her bus and was late for class. When she got to class, no one was there. She had to check her phone to see if there was an email from the instructor.
Take a moment and view this scenario through the lens of the internet of things.
With the Internet of Things
Since it was a really cold morning outside, the sensors on Susan's bedroom window alerted her electric blanket to turn up the heat to keep her warm. When Susan's alarm activated, the lights in her room turned on slowly to wake her up and the sensors turned off her electric blanket. The sensors in her apartment turned on the heating in her flat. The flat was well lit, Susan could see the dining room chair (and miss it) in her path to rush out the door. As Susan rushed passed her cat and the cat dishes, she could see the cat feeder dispensed food and fresh water. Once she locked her door, all of lighting and heating turned off, and the cat door unlocked to allow Fluffy, the cat, to go outside. Susan ran to the bus stop because her watch alerted her that the bus was about to arrive to her bus stop and that she might be late for it. Luckily, she made it on time and as a reward an alert popped up onto Susan's watch and offered her a free coffee at the student hub at her university. As Susan exited the bus, she received a notification from her instructor that her class venue had changed and informed her of its new location and due to the change, the class will start fifteen minutes later. Susan messaged her instructor she would attend on time. Susan's friend, Molly, messaged her and asked her to meet for a quick coffee before class because Molly received notification that Susan made her bus on time too. Susan smiled and thought – 'free coffee'.
Analysis:
The sensors in the everyday things in Susan's apartment 'sensed' her activity. The temperature sensors on her window communicated with her electric blanket and heating system in her apartment. The sensors on Susan's cat feeder activated upon her waking. The sensors on Susan's door communicated with the bus to determine if Susan would make the bus on time, using geolocation sensors on her watch and sensors on the bus she was meant to take. Since Susan made the bus on time, her institution knew she would arrive on time to university based on the notification sent from her bus to her institution. As a reward, her institution sent her a free coffee coupon. Also, Susan's instructor alerted the students that the class venue had changed. Susan communicated with her instructor and her friend Molly using the social media affordances from her watch or based on the connectedness of the things that monitored her activity.
Privacy issues aside, the things in Susan's life communicated in real-time with each other in her home, on her way to the bus and at her institution and based on this activity her friend and instructor communicated with her.
This provides an example of what the sensors in everyday things can do. The things (and people) in her life are 'context aware' and communicate with each other based on Susan's activities.

alert, notify, or serve content to users in a relevant and timely fashion. While the Internet of Things is not specifically a social media application, having the things in everyday life connected in combination with social media applications or that offer social media affordances can provide more opportunities for the growth of social media in students' lives. For example, in the vignette, it is a future possibility for Susan's institution to send her a coffee coupon for making her bus to arrive on time; in this case the IOT is "context aware" and recognized Susan's behavior patterns (Adams Becker, Cummins, et al., 2017; Whitmore, Agarwal, & Da Xu, 2015). A combination of mathematical formulas, algorithms, noting Susan's behavior and timings were all considered and prompted the free coffee offer in the example. A real-life example, cited in the NMC Horizon Report: 2017 Higher Education edition, is the ability for Virginia Tech to send emergency notifications to students through their smartwatches or smartphones (Adams Becker, Cumins, et al., 2017). Tremendous 'hype' surrounds the possibilities for social media and affordances for the IOT. How the IOT might be implemented in higher education in the social media landscape remains in its infancy.

Different Realities: Augmented and Virtual

The proliferation and availability of content through social media programs and applications and the ubiquity of user-generated context, through use of these programs, is on the rise (Meeker, 2017; Molla, 2017). Augmented reality is a mixed reality of real world and digital content. It is digital content infused into a real-world environment, not real-world content into a virtual environment (Bower, Howe, McCredie, Robinson, & Grover, 2014). An example of augmented reality is the process of placing biometric inputs through facial recognition software that can superimpose masks, muscles, emoticons and other digital visual elements or cartoon face filters in Instagram and Snapchat (Meeker, 2017). Consider the possibility of augmented reality program that overlays facial muscles over a student's face in live streamed video for an anatomy class. The instructor can ask students to observe the mechanics of facial muscles as a student smiles, frowns and chews. Instagram and Facebook and others currently offer this technology for its use with augmented reality overlays. The augmented reality offers different opportunities for how students interact with each other in a social way in a variety of contexts.

Virtual reality, on the other hand, immerses students in a completely virtual 3D computer generated environment (Gregory et al., 2012, 2013; Merchant, Goetz, Cifuentes, Keeney-Kennicutt, & Davis, 2014). Usually stereoscopic goggles and sometimes gloves with sensors are used to immerse students in these environments (Gregory et al., 2012, 2013; Merchant et al., 2014). Virtual reality can involve a 3D experience interacting with artifacts in an artificially generated environment or can involve interaction with others sometimes as an avatar, located in a different location (Gregory et al., 2012, 2013; Merchant et al., 2014). Imagine a virtual reality classroom in which students from different physical locations in the world can interact and physically hand each other objects in a virtual classroom space. Since 1979 virtual reality has been used in higher education and examples of this use include collaborative architecture studios in which students collaborate and build virtual homes; full immersion environments for foreign language learning; role playing scenarios; experimentation; simulation, and dialogic interaction in the virtual reality program Second Life and many more (Gregory et al., 2012). The virtual reality environment can offer many of the affordances that social media can offer in terms of co-creativity and co-collaboration within a live context regardless of physical locale.

Facebook has currently released a test version of Facebook Spaces a 3D virtual reality program that enables its users to interact with each other in alternate virtual locations and universes based on a user's current Facebook uses and preferences (Kelly & Larson, 2017). For example, users within the virtual space can choose artificially generated cartoon-character like avatars and interact with each other by using and sharing objects like markers, pens and even a selfie-stick for taking photos (Kelly & Larson, 2017). Users can also choose to use environments that reflect their 'interests', such as location in space or a tourist destination, such as the Philippines (Kelly & Larson, 2017). Facebook, the largest social media network, will be able to offer Facebook Spaces through its massive base of users worldwide which will eventually become widely available (Chaffey, 2017; Kelly & Larson, 2017). Imagine conducting class in a Facebook Space course with students on the moon simulating moving and working in low gravity. As this is emergent technology, much of the speculation is hype, yet to be tested and researched for use in higher education.

Gamification and Gamified Learning

Over time, online gaming has evolved from individual play to global collaborative play. Interactive gaming is on the rise worldwide with approximately 2.6 billion gamers as of 2017 with China now listed the top market for interactive gaming (Meeker, 2017; Molla, 2017). The affordances of social media are now prevalent throughout these gaming programs. These affordances can include, live chats, messaging, group forums, and more. Social media tools once set aside for traditional social media platforms are now integrated into the gaming technologies connecting players with others around the world enabling social engagement and real-time game play (Meeker, 2017; Molla, 2017).

Gamification involves the use of game-like mechanics and game design elements in non-game contexts, for example making a game out of learning a foreign language (Pappas, 2015). The mobile application DuoLingo gamifies the learning of foreign languages through quizzes, charts, and comparisons with other players, for example. Gamification transforms the learning requirements and tasks into an encouragement activity, quests, point systems, leader boards, badges, and progression levels provide examples of elements present in gamification (Pappas, 2015; Teach Thought Staff, 2014). Examples of educational gamification technologies that are already being used in tertiary education include Kahoot, Duolingo, and others. Kahoot provides opportunities for live game-based quizzes in the classroom enabling social collaborative interactions for students and social media platforms, like Facebook, offer their own on-line games through which the user can play with other Facebook users around the world.

Gamified learning, on the other hand, uses a pre-existing game to learn specific skills or processes (Pappas, 2015; Teach Thought Staff, 2014). Tannahill, Tissington, and Senior conclude from their research on the video game "Call of Duty" that video gaming offers constructivist gaming structures such as making failures learning opportunities, encouraging thinking about systems, and providing consistent just in time feedback and mental and motivational stimulation (2012). "Call of Duty" is a World War 2 simulation game that enables gamers to play the game in multiple theaters of war including the American, Russian, and British theaters with the aim of winning assigned objectives and battles in collaboration with your fellow "squad" soldiers (Infinity Ward, Treyarch, & Sledgehammer Games, 2003). World of Warcraft, Diablo, Starcraft and Overwatch are some of the largest collaborative online games available today (Meeker, 2017). Meeker describes online video gaming as the "most engaging" form of social media available (Meeker, 2017).

The advantages in using gamification and gamified learning are the alternative activities that enable student to engage with content as a game. Through various types of social gaming techniques, competition, team competition, students are encouraged to persist through failure, and co-operate to succeed attributes that are valued in both higher education and employment. Many of these techniques offer social media affordances, of student social interaction and collaboration and even offer students the ability to scale the privacy of their interactions and audiences. Students will not want to alert their next move to the enemy in a game, for example. These new technologies and their social media affordances possess significant potential for use in teaching and learning practice in higher education.

FUTURE RESEARCH DIRECTIONS

Emerging social media technologies, will most likely continue to be relevant and timely for tertiary education. As the technologies change and shift, so can the practices and modalities of delivery in education. Social media allows dynamic and fluid practice of teaching and learning that can be adapted to fit institutions. That is, it can be changed to be purpose fit for students' learning needs, teachers, best practice, teaching pedagogies and institutional requirements. Further research into the personalization aspects of social media at the student, instructional, and institutional levels would assist in understanding how social media and its affordances can be suited to unique requirements. As the support technologies as the IOT evolve and the social media affordances become available through them, further research in this technology and how it might impact higher education is warranted. Additionally, continued research into educational and social applications of virtual and augmented realities and gamified learning and gamification will need to continue since these technologies are continuing to evolve and instructors and institutions are choosing to utilize them in multiple ways. The more mobile, personal and connected social media technologies and affordances become, so too will our notions and understanding of connectedness and learning. Institutions, instructors and students will continue to navigate this space as while attempting to continue to protect personal privacy and data. Further research in the areas of student privacy and data should continue. Regardless of the technologies or practices used for social media applications in higher education, it is suggested that further research into social learning opportunities and activities should be conducted designed for further understanding of the dynamics of co-creation and co-collaboration can be identified through the social media affordances utilized.

CONCLUSION

Higher education courses will continue to engage with students in face to face and blended learning networks and environments. Emergent social media technologies can provide co-collaborative and co-creative opportunities for students now and in the future. While the modalities of delivery and may change, emergent social media technologies should be designed with pedagogical purposes in mind, offer students social and co-creative opportunities in real life or authentic contexts. While the future cannot be predicted, further research into the current state and use of social media technologies is required to obtain further understanding and possible future directions. Truly, all ideas and suggestions in this chapter, since emergent and in most cases, in a dynamic state, should continue to be researched to shed light on new possibilities and potential for social media and its affordances in higher education. It is indisputable is that social media and social media affordances of emergent technologies will continue to appear in the teaching and learning landscape as well as provide tremendous potential for higher education.

REFERENCES

Adams Becker, S., Cummins, M., Davis, A., Freeman, A., Hall Giesinger, C., & Ananthanarayanan, V. (2017). *NMC horizon report: 2017 higher education edition*. Austin, TX: The New Media Consortium.

Afreen, R. (2014). Bring your own device (BYOD) in higher education: Opportunities and challenges. *International Journal of Emerging Trends & Technology in Computer Science, 3*(1), 233–236.

Bower, M., Howe, C., McCredie, N., Robinson, A., & Grover, D. (2014). Augmented reality in education – cases, places and potentials. *Educational Media International, 51*(1), 1–15. doi:10.1080/09523987.2014.889400

Brooks, D. C. (2016). *ECAR study of undergraduate students and information technology*. Retrieved from https://library.educause.edu/resources/2016/6/~/media/files/library/2016/10/ers1605.pdf

Brown, J. L. (2017, March 23). *How will the internet of things impact education?* Retrieved October 11, 2017, from https://edtechmagazine.com/k12/article/2017/03/how-will-internet-things-impact-education

Callan, V. J., Johnston, M. A., & Poulsen, A. L. (2015). How organisations are using blended e-learning to deliver more flexible approaches to trade training. *Journal of Vocational Education and Training, 67*(3), 294–309. doi:10.1080/13636820.2015.1050445

Chaffey, D. (2017, April 27). *Global social media statistics summary 2017.* Retrieved September 14, 2017, from http://www.smartinsights.com/social-media-marketing/social-media-strategy/new-global-social-media-research/

DeMers, J. (2017, January 23). *Does your social media app know too much about you?* Retrieved October 26, 2017, from https://www.forbes.com/sites/jaysondemers/2017/01/23/does-your-social-media-app-know-too-much-about-you/

Gregory, S., Gregory, B., Hillier, M., Jacka, L., Farley, H., Stokes-Thompson, F., ... Scutter, S. (2012). Sustaining the future through virtual worlds. Future Challenges, Sustainable Futures. *Proceedings Ascilite, 2012,* 361–368.

Gregory, S., Gregory, B., Reiners, T., Fardinpour, A., Hillier, M., & Lee, M. (2013). *Virtual worlds in Australian and New Zealand higher education: Remembering the past, understanding the present and imagining the future.* Retrieved from https://eprints.qut.edu.au/64096/

Helman, B. (2014). Bring everything: BYOD's evolution in higher education. *Information Week,* 1.

Hew, K. F., & Cheung, W. S. (2013). Use of Web 2.0 technologies in K-12 and higher education: The search for evidence-based practice. *Educational Research Review, 9,* 47–64. doi:10.1016/j.edurev.2012.08.001

Hootsuite Media, Inc. (2017, October). *2017 social campus report.* Retrieved October 19, 2017, from https://hootsuite.com/resources/social-campus-report

Jacobsson, S. (2010, May 20). *Social networking sites may be sharing your info with advertisers.* Retrieved October 26, 2017, from https://www.pcworld.com/article/196869/Social_Network_Privacy.html

Kelly, H., & Larson, S. (2017, April 18). *Facebook finally makes a virtual reality world.* Retrieved November 8, 2017, from http://money.cnn.com/2017/04/18/technology/facebook-f8/index.html

Manca, S., & Ranieri, M. (2016). Facebook and the others. Potentials and obstacles of social media for teaching in higher education. *Computers & Education, 95*(Supplement C), 216–230. doi:10.1016/j.compedu.2016.01.012

Meeker, M. (2017, May). *2017 internet trends report.* Presented at the Code Conference, Rancho Palos Verdes, CA. Retrieved from http://www.kpcb.com/internet-trends

Meola, A. (2016, December 20). *How IoT in education is changing the way we learn.* Retrieved October 11, 2017, from http://www.businessinsider.com/internet-of-things-education-2016-9

Merchant, Z., Goetz, E. T., Cifuentes, L., Keeney-Kennicutt, W., & Davis, T. J. (2014). Effectiveness of virtual reality-based instruction on students' learning outcomes in K-12 and higher education: A meta-analysis. *Computers & Education, 70,* 29–40. doi:10.1016/j.compedu.2013.07.033

Molla, R. (2017, May 31). *Mary Meeker's 2017 internet trends report: All the slides, plus analysis.* Retrieved October 7, 2017, from https://www.recode.net/2017/5/31/15693686/mary-meeker-kleiner-perkins-kpcb-slides-internet-trends-code-2017

Newman, T., & Beetham, H. (2017). *Student digital experience tracker report 2017.* JISC. Retrieved from http://repository.jisc.ac.uk/6662/

Nore, H. (2015). Re-Contextualizing vocational didactics in Norwegian vocational education and training. *International Journal for Research in Vocational Education and Training, 2*(3), 182–194.

Palmer, J., & Strickland, J. (2017, February). *Academic social networking websites.* Retrieved November 4, 2017, from http://www.apa.org/science/about/psa/2017/02/academic-social-networking.aspx

Pappas, C. (2015, April 20). *Gamification vs game-based eLearning: Can you tell the difference?* Retrieved October 14, 2017, from https://elearningindustry.com/gamification-vs-game-based-elearning-can-you-tell-the-difference

Parsons, D. (2014). The future of mobile learning and implications for education and training. In *Increasing access through mobile learning* (Vol. 217, pp. 217–229). Vancouver, Canada: Commonwealth of Learning (COL); Athabasca University. Retrieved from http://oasis.col.org/bitstream/handle/11599/558/pub_Mobile%20Learning_web.pdf#page=234

Reisenwitz, C. (2017, October 16). *9 doctor social networking sites every physician should know about.* Retrieved November 4, 2017, from https://blog.capterra.com/9-doctor-social-networking-sites-every-physician-should-know-about/

Roman, J. (2011). *BYOD: Manage the risks*. Retrieved from http://www. bankinfosecurity.in/interviews/byod-manage-risks-i-1327

Siddiqui, R. (2014). Bring your own device (BYOD) in higher education: Opportunities and challenges. *International Journal of Emerging Trends & Technology in Computer Science, 3*, 233–236.

Tannahill, N., Tissington, P., & Senior, C. (2012). Video games and higher education: What can "Call of Duty" teach our students? *Frontiers in Psychology, 3*. doi:10.3389/fpsyg.2012.00210 PMID:22737142

Teach Thought Staff. (2014, April 4). *The difference between gamification and game-based learning*. Retrieved October 14, 2017, from https://www. teachthought.com/learning/difference-gamification-game-based-learning/

Tess, P. A. (2013). The role of social media in higher education classes (real and virtual) – A literature review. *Computers in Human Behavior, 29*(5), A60–A68. doi:10.1016/j.chb.2012.12.032

UNESCO. (Ed.). (2016). *Education for people and planet: creating sustainable futures for all* (2nd ed.). Paris: UNESCO.

United Nations. (2017). *World population prospects: The 2017 revision, key findings and advance tables* (No. ESA/P/WP/248). Retrieved from https:// esa.un.org/unpd/wpp/Publications/Files/WPP2017_KeyFindings.pdf

Van Leeuwen, D. (2014). Bring your own software. *Network Security, 2014*(3), 12–13. doi:10.1016/S1353-4858(14)70031-5

Veletsianos, G. (2010). Part 1 - Foundations of emerging technologies in distance education. In *Emerging technologies in distance education* (pp. 1–22). AU Press. Retrieved from http://eds.a.ebscohost.com.ezproxy.massey. ac.nz/eds/ebookviewer/ebook/bmxlYmtfXzMzNzUzM19fQU41?sid=ef0e 3e37-319e-4d45-a1f9-56a64f9080d4@sessionmgr4006&vid=0&format= EB&rid=1

Veletsianos, G. (2016). The defining characteristics of emerging technologies and emerging practices in digital education. *Emergence and Innovation in Digital Learning: Foundations and Applications*.

Ward, I. Treyarch, & Sledgehammer Games. (2003). *Call of duty*. Santa Monica, CA: Activision. Retrieved from https://www.activision.com/

Whitmore, A., Agarwal, A., & Da Xu, L. (2015). The internet of things—A survey of topics and trends. *Information Systems Frontiers*, *17*(2), 261–274. doi:10.100710796-014-9489-2

KEY TERMS AND DEFINITIONS

Affordances: The ability or abilities of the technologies used. For example, a digital camera on a smartphone can record sound, take images, and digital video; those are the affordances of the digital camera.

Augmented Reality: The use of digital overlays like emoticons, drawings, or images combined with digital video or images.

Avatar: A character, shape, or icon that can represent a person in a computer environment.

BYOE: Bring your own everything policy. It is a policy that encourages allows to use their own devices and software at their educational institutions.

Gamification: Involves the use of game-like mechanics and game design elements in non-game contexts, for example making a game out of learning a foreign language.

Gamified Learning: Uses a pre-existing game to learn specific skills or processes.

Internet of Things: Technology that can make everyday items connectable to other devices and the internet.

Virtual Reality: A world generated in a 3D computer environment that can be engaged in by using specialty equipment such as headsets, goggles, and gloves equipped with special sensors.

Related Readings

To continue IGI Global's long-standing tradition of advancing innovation through emerging research, please find below a compiled list of recommended IGI Global book chapters and journal articles in the areas of teaching practices, social media, and curriculum integration. These related readings will provide additional information and guidance to further enrich your knowledge and assist you with your own research.

Abdelaziz, H. A. (2014). Creative Design of Interactive eLearning Activities and Materials (IEAM): A Psycho-Pedagogical Model. *International Journal of Technology Diffusion*, 5(4), 14–34. doi:10.4018/ijtd.2014100102

Abdelmalak, M. M., & Parra, J. L. (2016). Expanding Learning Opportunities for Graduate Students with HyFlex Course Design. *International Journal of Online Pedagogy and Course Design*, 6(4), 19–37. doi:10.4018/IJOPCD.2016100102

Abera, B. (2014). Applying a Technological Pedagogical Content Knowledge Framework in Ethiopian English Language Teacher Education. In T. Issa, P. Isaias, & P. Kommers (Eds.), Multicultural Awareness and Technology in Higher Education: Global Perspectives (pp. 286–301). Hershey, PA: IGI Global. doi:10.4018/978-1-4666-5876-9.ch014

Adegbenro, J. B., Gumbo, M. T., & Olugbara, O. O. (2015). Exploring Technological Knowledge of Office Data Processing Teachers: Using Factor Analytic Methods. In M. Niess & H. Gillow-Wiles (Eds.), Handbook of Research on Teacher Education in the Digital Age (pp. 548–576). Hershey, PA: IGI Global. doi:10.4018/978-1-4666-8403-4.ch021

Amador, F., Nobre, A., & Barros, D. (2016). Towards a Model of a Didactics of eLearning: An Application to Education for Sustainable Development. In M. Pinheiro & D. Simões (Eds.), Handbook of Research on Engaging Digital Natives in Higher Education Settings (pp. 396–415). Hershey, PA: IGI Global. doi:10.4018/978-1-5225-0039-1.ch019

Amador, J. M., Kimmons, R., Miller, B. G., Desjardins, C. D., & Hall, C. (2015). Preparing Preservice Teachers to Become Self-Reflective of Their Technology Integration Practices. In M. Niess & H. Gillow-Wiles (Eds.), Handbook of Research on Teacher Education in the Digital Age (pp. 81–107). Hershey, PA: IGI Global. doi:10.4018/978-1-4666-8403-4.ch004

Archambault, L. (2014). Teaching Virtually: Strategies and Challenges in the 21st Century Online Classroom. *International Journal of Online Pedagogy and Course Design*, 4(1), 1–15. doi:10.4018/ijopcd.2014010101

Arinze, B., Sylla, C., & Amobi, O. (2016). Cloud Computing for Teaching and Learning: Design Strategies. In L. Chao (Ed.), Handbook of Research on Cloud-Based STEM Education for Improved Learning Outcomes (pp. 159–171). Hershey, PA: IGI Global. doi:10.4018/978-1-4666-9924-3.ch011

Aşık, A. (2016). Digital Storytelling and Its Tools for Language Teaching: Perceptions and Reflections of Pre-Service Teachers. *International Journal of Computer-Assisted Language Learning and Teaching*, 6(1), 55–68. doi:10.4018/IJCALLT.2016010104

Attard, C. (2015). Introducing iPads into Primary Mathematics Classrooms: Teachers' Experiences and Pedagogies. In M. Meletiou-Mavrotheris, K. Mavrou, & E. Paparistodemou (Eds.), Integrating Touch-Enabled and Mobile Devices into Contemporary Mathematics Education (pp. 193–213). Hershey, PA: IGI Global. doi:10.4018/978-1-4666-8714-1.ch009

Baert, H. (2015). Technology Tools, Proficiency, and Integration of Physical Education Teacher Educators. In M. Niess & H. Gillow-Wiles (Eds.), Handbook of Research on Teacher Education in the Digital Age (pp. 223–254). Hershey, PA: IGI Global. doi:10.4018/978-1-4666-8403-4.ch009

Banas, J. R., & York, C. S. (2014). The Impact of Authentic Learning Exercises On Pre-service Teachers' Motivational Beliefs towards Technology Integration. *International Journal of Information and Communication Technology Education*, 10(3), 60–76. doi:10.4018/ijicte.2014070105

Barakat, M., & Weiss-Randall, D. N. (2016). Through the Eyes of Students and Faculty: A Conceptual Framework for the Development of Online Courses. In V. Wang (Ed.), Handbook of Research on Learning Outcomes and Opportunities in the Digital Age (pp. 557–584). Hershey, PA: IGI Global. doi:10.4018/978-1-4666-9577-1.ch025

Baran, M. L., & Jones, J. E. (2014). Online Learning: Guidelines for Team Effectiveness. In C. Stevenson & J. Bauer (Eds.), Building Online Communities in Higher Education Institutions: Creating Collaborative Experience (pp. 279–292). Hershey, PA: IGI Global. doi:10.4018/978-1-4666-5178-4.ch015

Barbour, M. K., Adelstein, D., & Morrison, J. (2014). The Forgotten Teachers in K-12 Online Learning: Examining the Perceptions of Teachers Who Develop K-12 Online Courses. *International Journal of Online Pedagogy and Course Design*, *4*(3), 18–33. doi:10.4018/ijopcd.2014070102

Boboc, M. (2014). Connecting Communication to Curriculum and Pedagogy in Online Environments. In C. Stevenson & J. Bauer (Eds.), Building Online Communities in Higher Education Institutions: Creating Collaborative Experience (pp. 132–156). Hershey, PA: IGI Global. doi:10.4018/978-1-4666-5178-4.ch007

Borasi, R., Fredericksen, E., & Miller, D. (2017). From 0 to 60: The Case Study of a School of Education's Successful "Online Start-Up". In K. Shelton & K. Pedersen (Eds.), *Handbook of Research on Building* (pp. 60–83). Hershey, PA: IGI Global. doi:10.4018/978-1-5225-0877-9.ch004

Bowers, J., & Kumar, P. (2015). Students' Perceptions of Teaching and Social Presence: A Comparative Analysis of Face-to-Face and Online Learning Environments. *International Journal of Web-Based Learning and Teaching Technologies*, *10*(1), 27–44. doi:10.4018/ijwltt.2015010103

Bozoglan, B., & Demirer, V. (2015). The Association between Internet Addiction and Psychosocial Variables. In J. Bishop (Ed.), Psychological and Social Implications Surrounding Internet and Gaming Addiction (pp. 171–185). Hershey, PA: IGI Global: IGI Global. doi:10.4018/978-1-4666-8595-6.ch010

Breen, P. (2014). Philosophies, Traditional Pedagogy, and New Technologies: A Report on a Case Study of EAP Teachers' Integration of Technology into Traditional Practice. In P. Breen (Ed.), *Cases on Teacher Identity* (pp. 317–341). Hershey, PA: IGI Global. doi:10.4018/978-1-4666-5990-2.ch013

Brockmeier, F. (2017). Service Learning Online: Preparing to Work in Global Societies with E-Service-Learning. In C. Crosby & F. Brockmeier (Eds.), *Student Experiences and Educational Outcomes in Community Engagement for the 21st Century* (pp. 150–172). Hershey, PA: IGI Global. doi:10.4018/978-1-5225-0874-8.ch007

Brunvand, S. (2016). Facilitating Student Interaction and Collaboration in a MOOC Environment. In R. Mendoza-Gonzalez (Ed.), *User-Centered Design Strategies for Massive Open Online Courses (MOOCs)* (pp. 1–14). Hershey, PA: IGI Global. doi:10.4018/978-1-4666-9743-0.ch001

Bull, P. H., & Patterson, G. C. (2016). Strategies to Promote Pedagogical Knowledge Interplay with Technology. In J. Keengwe & G. Onchwari (Eds.), *Handbook of Research on Active Learning and the Flipped Classroom Model in the Digital Age* (pp. 255–271). Hershey, PA: IGI Global. doi:10.4018/978-1-4666-9680-8.ch013

Bush, S. B., Driskell, S. O., Niess, M. L., Pugalee, D., Rakes, C. R., & Ronau, R. N. (2015). The Impact of Digital Technologies in Mathematics Pre-Service Teacher Preparation over Four Decades. In M. Niess & H. Gillow-Wiles (Eds.), *Handbook of Research on Teacher Education in the Digital Age* (pp. 1–27). Hershey, PA: IGI Global. doi:10.4018/978-1-4666-8403-4.ch001

Byrd-Poller, L., Farmer, J. L., & Ford, V. (2017). The Role of Leaders in Facilitating Healing After Organizational Trauma. In S. Háša & R. Brunet-Thornton (Eds.), *Impact of Organizational Trauma on Workplace Behavior and Performance* (pp. 318–340). Hershey, PA: IGI Global. doi:10.4018/978-1-5225-2021-4.ch014

Cacho-Elizondo, S., Shahidi, N., & Tossan, V. (2015). Giving Up Smoking Using SMS Messages on your Mobile Phone. In A. Mesquita & C. Tsai (Eds.), *Human Behavior, Psychology, and Social Interaction in the Digital Era* (pp. 72–94). Hershey, PA: IGI Global. doi:10.4018/978-1-4666-8450-8.ch004

Card, S., & Wang, H. (2015). Taking Care to Play: Meaningful Communication in Dementia Care in Chinese Culture. In C. Dick-Muehlke, R. Li, & M. Orleans (Eds.), *Psychosocial Studies of the Individual's Changing Perspectives in Alzheimer's Disease* (pp. 76–103). Hershey, PA: IGI Global. doi:10.4018/978-1-4666-8478-2.ch004

Carrasco, G., & Kinnamon, E. (2017). An Examination of Selfish and Selfless Motives: A Review of the Social Psychological and Behavioral Economics Literature. In R. Ianole (Ed.), *Applied Behavioral Economics Research and Trends* (pp. 93–109). Hershey, PA: IGI Global. doi:10.4018/978-1-5225-1826-6.ch006

Cejka, P., & Mohelska, H. (2017). National Culture Influence on Organisational Trauma: A Conceptual Framework Review. In S. Háša & R. Brunet-Thornton (Eds.), *Impact of Organizational Trauma on Workplace Behavior and Performance* (pp. 162–186). Hershey, PA: IGI Global. doi:10.4018/978-1-5225-2021-4.ch007

Chen, C. (2016). Effective Learning Strategies for the 21st Century: Implications for the E-Learning. In M. Anderson & C. Gavan (Eds.), *Developing Effective Educational Experiences through Learning Analytics* (pp. 143–169). Hershey, PA: IGI Global. doi:10.4018/978-1-4666-9983-0.ch006

Chen, C., Chiu, P., & Huang, Y. (2015). The Learning Style-Based Adaptive Learning System Architecture. *International Journal of Online Pedagogy and Course Design*, *5*(2), 1–10. doi:10.4018/IJOPCD.2015040101

Chen, R., Lin, T., & Xie, T. (2015). Towards Intelligent Window Layout Management: The Role of Mental Map. In A. Mesquita & C. Tsai (Eds.), *Human Behavior, Psychology, and Social Interaction in the Digital Era* (pp. 146–161). Hershey, PA: IGI Global. doi:10.4018/978-1-4666-8450-8.ch007

Cheng, H. (2017). A TL-TPACK Model on CSL Pre-Service Teachers' Competencies of Online Instruction. In C. Lin, D. Zhang, & B. Zheng (Eds.), *Preparing Foreign Language Teachers for Next-Generation Education* (pp. 198–225). Hershey, PA: IGI Global. doi:10.4018/978-1-5225-0483-2.ch011

Chuang, S., Lin, S., Chang, T., & Kaewmeesri, R. (2017). Behavioral Intention of Using Social Networking Site: A Comparative Study of Taiwanese and Thai Facebook Users. *International Journal of Technology and Human Interaction*, *13*(1), 61–81. doi:10.4018/IJTHI.2017010104

Cialdella, V. T., Lobato, E. J., & Jordan, J. S. (2017). Wild Architecture: Explaining Cognition via Self-Sustaining Systems. In J. Vallverdú, M. Mazzara, M. Talanov, S. Distefano, & R. Lowe (Eds.), *Advanced Research on Biologically Inspired Cognitive Architectures* (pp. 41–62). Hershey, PA: IGI Global. doi:10.4018/978-1-5225-1947-8.ch003

Çınar, M., & Tüzün, H. (2016). Web-Based Course Design Models. In M. Pinheiro & D. Simões (Eds.), *Handbook of Research on Engaging Digital Natives in Higher Education Settings* (pp. 374–395). Hershey, PA: IGI Global. doi:10.4018/978-1-5225-0039-1.ch018

Cleve, R. A., Işık, İ., & Pecanha, V. D. (2017). Sexual Identities in the Workplace: Avoiding Organizational Trauma When Disclosure Occurs – Current Perspectives. In S. Háša & R. Brunet-Thornton (Eds.), *Impact of Organizational Trauma on Workplace Behavior and Performance* (pp. 188–220). Hershey, PA: IGI Global. doi:10.4018/978-1-5225-2021-4.ch008

Conrad, S. S., & Dabbagh, N. (2015). Examining the Factors that Influence how Instructors Provide Feedback in Online Learning Environments. *International Journal of Online Pedagogy and Course Design*, 5(4), 47–66. doi:10.4018/IJOPCD.2015100104

Contier, A. T., & Torres, L. (2017). Neuroaesthetics: Insights into the Aesthetic Experience of Visual Art. In R. Zuanon (Ed.), *Projective Processes and Neuroscience in Art and Design* (pp. 87–102). Hershey, PA: IGI Global. doi:10.4018/978-1-5225-0510-5.ch006

Courey, S., LePage, P., Blackorby, J., Siker, J., & Nguyen, T. (2015). The Effects of Using Dynabook to Prepare Special Education Teachers to Teach Proportional Reasoning. *International Journal of Web-Based Learning and Teaching Technologies*, 10(1), 45–64. doi:10.4018/ijwltt.2015010104

Cranton, P., & Thompson, P. (2014). Creating Collaboration in Global Online Learning: Case Studies. In V. Wang (Ed.), *Handbook of Research on Education and Technology in a Changing Society* (pp. 92–103). Hershey, PA: IGI Global. doi:10.4018/978-1-4666-6046-5.ch007

Crawford, C. M., & Smith, M. S. (2015). Rethinking Bloom's Taxonomy: Implicit Cognitive Vulnerability as an Impetus towards Higher Order Thinking Skills. In Z. Jin (Ed.), *Exploring Implicit Cognition: Learning, Memory, and Social Cognitive Processes* (pp. 86–103). Hershey, PA: IGI Global. doi:10.4018/978-1-4666-6599-6.ch004

de Groot, C., Fogleman, J., & Kern, D. (2015). Using Mobile Technologies to Co-Construct TPACK in Teacher Education. In J. Keengwe & M. Maxfield (Eds.), *Advancing Higher Education with Mobile Learning Technologies: Cases* (pp. 195–219). Hershey, PA: IGI Global. doi:10.4018/978-1-4666-6284-1.ch011 de Soir, E., & Kleber, R. (2017). Understanding the Core of Psychological Trauma: Trauma in Contemporary French Theory. In S. Háša & R. Brunet-Thornton (Eds.), *Impact of Organizational Trauma on Workplace Behavior and Performance* (pp. 57–75). Hershey, PA: IGI Global. doi:10.4018/978-1-5225-2021-4.ch003

Delgado, J. J. (2017). How Is the Personality of Facebook Customers?: Cloninger's Psychobiological Model of Temperament as a Predictor of SNSs. In M. Dos Santos (Ed.), *Applying Neuroscience to Business Practice* (pp. 191–229). Hershey, PA: IGI Global. doi:10.4018/978-1-5225-1028-4.ch009

Dentale, F., Vecchione, M., & Barbaranelli, C. (2015). Applying the IAT to Assess Big Five Personality Traits: A Brief Review of Measurement and Validity Issues. In Z. Jin (Ed.), *Exploring Implicit Cognition: Learning, Memory, and Social Cognitive Processes* (pp. 1–15). Hershey, PA: IGI Global. doi:10.4018/978-1-4666-6599-6.ch001

Deyoe, M. M., Newman, D. L., & Asaro-Saddler, K. (2014). Moving from Professional Development to Real-Time Use: How are we Changing Students? In J. Keengwe, G. Onchwari, & D. Hucks (Eds.), *Literacy Enrichment and Technology Integration in Pre-Service Teacher Education* (pp. 160–182). Hershey, PA: IGI Global. doi:10.4018/978-1-4666-4924-8.ch010

Dick, T. P., & Burrill, G. F. (2016). Design and Implementation Principles for Dynamic Interactive Mathematics Technologies. In M. Niess, S. Driskell, & K. Hollebrands (Eds.), *Handbook of Research on Transforming Mathematics Teacher Education in the Digital Age* (pp. 23–51). Hershey, PA: IGI Global. doi:10.4018/978-1-5225-0120-6.ch002

Díez, J. C., & Saiz-Alvarez, J. M. (2016). Leadership in Social Entrepreneurship: Is It Ability or Skill? In J. Saiz-Álvarez (Ed.), *Handbook of Research on Social Entrepreneurship and Solidarity Economics* (pp. 134–153). Hershey, PA: IGI Global. doi:10.4018/978-1-5225-0097-1.ch008

Dikici, A. (2017). Revisiting the Relationships between Turkish Prospective Teachers' Thinking Styles and Behaviors Fostering Creativity. In N. Silton (Ed.), *Exploring the Benefits of Creativity in Education, Media, and the Arts* (pp. 136–157). Hershey, PA: IGI Global. doi:10.4018/978-1-5225-0504-4.ch007

Dodd, B. J., Baukal, C. E. Jr, & Ausburn, L. J. (2016). A Post-Positivist Framework for Using and Building Theory in Online Instructional Design. *International Journal of Online Pedagogy and Course Design*, 6(4), 53–70. doi:10.4018/IJOPCD.2016100104

Driskell, S. O., Bush, S. B., Ronau, R. N., Niess, M. L., Rakes, C. R., & Pugalee, D. K. (2016). Mathematics Education Technology Professional Development: Changes over Several Decades. In M. Niess, S. Driskell, & K. Hollebrands (Eds.), *Handbook of Research on Transforming Mathematics Teacher Education in the Digital Age* (pp. 107–136). Hershey, PA: IGI Global. doi:10.4018/978-1-5225-0120-6.ch005

Dunston, Y. L., Patterson, G. C., & Bull, P. H. (2016). Faculty Perspectives of Technology-Enhanced Course Redesign. In J. Keengwe & G. Onchwari (Eds.), *Handbook of Research on Active Learning and the Flipped Classroom Model in the Digital Age* (pp. 150–176). Hershey, PA: IGI Global. doi:10.4018/978-1-4666-9680-8.ch008

Duvall, M., Matranga, A., Foster, A., & Silverman, J. (2016). Mobile Learning: Technology as Mediator of Personal and School Experiences. *International Journal of Game-Based Learning*, 6(1), 30–42. doi:10.4018/IJGBL.2016010103

Eapen, V., & Walter, A. (2016). Mind the Gap: Developmental Vulnerability and Mental Health. In R. Gopalan (Ed.), *Handbook of Research on Diagnosing, Treating, and Managing Intellectual Disabilities* (pp. 11–32). Hershey, PA: IGI Global. doi:10.4018/978-1-5225-0089-6.ch002

Edson, A. J., & Thomas, A. (2016). Transforming Preservice Mathematics Teacher Knowledge for and with the Enacted Curriculum: The Case of Digital Instructional Materials. In M. Niess, S. Driskell, & K. Hollebrands (Eds.), *Handbook of Research on Transforming Mathematics Teacher Education in the Digital Age* (pp. 215–240). Hershey, PA: IGI Global. doi:10.4018/978-1-5225-0120-6.ch009

Fallon, F. (2017). Integrated Information Theory (IIT) and Artificial Consciousness. In J. Vallverdú, M. Mazzara, M. Talanov, S. Distefano, & R. Lowe (Eds.), *Advanced Research on Biologically Inspired Cognitive Architectures* (pp. 1–23). Hershey, PA: IGI Global. doi:10.4018/978-1-5225-1947-8.ch001

Fang, L., & Ha, L. (2015). Do College Students Benefit from Their Social Media Experience?: Social Media Involvement and Its Impact on College Students' Self-Efficacy Perception. In A. Mesquita & C. Tsai (Eds.), *Human Behavior, Psychology, and Social Interaction in the Digital Era* (pp. 259–278). Hershey, PA: IGI Global. doi:10.4018/978-1-4666-8450-8.ch013

Farmer, L. (2014). Technology Impact on New Adult Behavior about Health Information. In V. Wang (Ed.), *Handbook of Research on Adult and Community Health Education: Tools, Trends, and Methodologies* (pp. 68–81). Hershey, PA: IGI Global. doi:10.4018/978-1-4666-6260-5.ch005

Fasko, D. (2017). Creativity in the Schools: Educational Changes Lately? In N. Silton (Ed.), *Exploring the Benefits of Creativity in Education, Media, and the Arts* (pp. 92–116). Hershey, PA: IGI Global. doi:10.4018/978-1-5225-0504-4.ch005

Fasso, W., Knight, C., & Knight, B. A. (2014). A Learner-Centered Design Framework for E-Learning. *International Journal of Online Pedagogy and Course Design*, *4*(4), 44–59. doi:10.4018/ijopcd.2014100104

Fazio, S., & Mitchell, D. B. (2015). Self-Preservation in Individuals with Alzheimer's Disease: Empirical Evidence and the Role of the Social Environment. In C. Dick-Muehlke, R. Li, & M. Orleans (Eds.), *Psychosocial Studies of the Individual's Changing Perspectives in Alzheimer's Disease* (pp. 183–207). Hershey, PA: IGI Global. doi:10.4018/978-1-4666-8478-2.ch008

Feitosa-Santana, C. (2017). Understanding How the Mind Works: The Neuroscience of Perception, Behavior, and Creativity. In R. Zuanon (Ed.), *Projective Processes and Neuroscience in Art and Design* (pp. 239–252). Hershey, PA: IGI Global. doi:10.4018/978-1-5225-0510-5.ch014

Felger, J., & Shafer, K. G. (2016). An Algebra Teacher's Instructional Decision-Making Process with GeoGebra: Thinking with a TPACK Mindset. In M. Niess, S. Driskell, & K. Hollebrands (Eds.), *Handbook of Research on Transforming Mathematics Teacher Education in the Digital Age* (pp. 493–518). Hershey, PA: IGI Global. doi:10.4018/978-1-5225-0120-6.ch019

Ferris, A. (2017). Creativity in the Emerging Adult. In N. Silton (Ed.), *Exploring the Benefits of Creativity in Education, Media, and the Arts* (pp. 26–49). Hershey, PA: IGI Global. doi:10.4018/978-1-5225-0504-4.ch002

Fife, E., Nelson, C. L., & Clarke, T. B. (2014). Online Technological Media in the Higher Education Classroom: An Exploratory Investigation of Varied Levels of Twitter Use. *International Journal of Online Pedagogy and Course Design*, *4*(2), 35–45. doi:10.4018/ijopcd.2014040103

Figg, C., & Jaipal-Jamani, K. (2015). Developing Teacher Knowledge about Gamification as an Instructional Strategy. In M. Niess & H. Gillow-Wiles (Eds.), *Handbook of Research on Teacher Education in the Digital Age* (pp. 663–690). Hershey, PA: IGI Global. doi:10.4018/978-1-4666-8403-4.ch025

Finger, G. (2015). Improving Initial Teacher Education in Australia: Solutions and Recommendations from the Teaching Teachers for the Future Project. In N. Ololube, P. Kpolovie, & L. Makewa (Eds.), *Handbook of Research on Enhancing Teacher Education with Advanced Instructional Technologies* (pp. 187–207). Hershey, PA: IGI Global. doi:10.4018/978-1-4666-8162-0.ch010

Flores, A., Park, J., & Bernhardt, S. A. (2016). Learning Mathematics and Technology through Inquiry, Cooperation, and Communication: A Learning Trajectory for Future Mathematics Teachers. In M. Niess, S. Driskell, & K. Hollebrands (Eds.), *Handbook of Research on Transforming Mathematics Teacher Education in the Digital Age* (pp. 324–352). Hershey, PA: IGI Global. doi:10.4018/978-1-5225-0120-6.ch013

Fogliano, F., & Oliveira, H. C. (2017). Neuroesthetics: Perspectives and Reflections. In R. Zuanon (Ed.), *Projective Processes and Neuroscience in Art and Design* (pp. 52–70). Hershey, PA: IGI Global. doi:10.4018/978-1-5225-0510-5.ch004

Fokides, E. (2016). Pre-Service Teachers, Computers, and ICT Courses: A Troubled Relationship. *International Journal of Information and Communication Technology Education*, *12*(4), 25–36. doi:10.4018/IJICTE.2016100103

Folk, J. R., & Eskenazi, M. A. (2017). Eye Movement Behavior and Individual Differences in Word Identification During Reading. In C. Was, F. Sansosti, & B. Morris (Eds.), *Eye-Tracking Technology Applications in Educational Research* (pp. 66–87). Hershey, PA: IGI Global. doi:10.4018/978-1-5225-1005-5.ch004

Foster, A., & Shah, M. (2016). Knew Me and New Me: Facilitating Student Identity Exploration and Learning through Game Integration. *International Journal of Gaming and Computer-Mediated Simulations*, 8(3), 39–58. doi:10.4018/IJGCMS.2016070103

Franco, M., Ortiz, T. V., Amorim, H. A., & Faber, J. (2017). Can We Induce a Cognitive Representation of a Prosthetic Arm by Means of Crossmodal Stimuli? In R. Zuanon (Ed.), *Projective Processes and Neuroscience in Art and Design* (pp. 182–204). Hershey, PA: IGI Global. doi:10.4018/978-1-5225-0510-5.ch011

Frazier, L. C., & Palmer, B. M. (2015). Effective Online Learning Begins with Effective Teacher Preparation. In T. Heafner, R. Hartshorne, & T. Petty (Eds.), *Exploring the Effectiveness of Online Education in K-12 Environments* (pp. 148–168). Hershey, PA: IGI Global. doi:10.4018/978-1-4666-6383-1.ch008

G., L. (2017). Psychosocial Intervention Studies for Street Children with Substance Abuse. In B. Prasad (Ed.), *Chronic Mental Illness and the Changing Scope of Intervention Strategies, Diagnosis, and Treatment* (pp. 237-257). Hershey, PA: IGI Global. doi:10.4018/978-1-5225-0519-8.ch013

Gallagher-Lepak, S., & Vandenhouten, C. (2016). E-Learning and Faculty Development in Higher Education: A Comprehensive Project. In B. Khan (Ed.), *Revolutionizing Modern Education through Meaningful E-Learning Implementation* (pp. 226–244). Hershey, PA: IGI Global. doi:10.4018/978-1-5225-0466-5.ch012

Gallego, J. (2017). Organizational Trauma and Change Management. In S. Háša & R. Brunet-Thornton (Eds.), *Impact of Organizational Trauma on Workplace Behavior and Performance* (pp. 140–161). Hershey, PA: IGI Global. doi:10.4018/978-1-5225-2021-4.ch006

Galvin, J. E., & Kelleher, M. E. (2015). Dementia and Other Neurocognitive Disorders: An Overview. In C. Dick-Muehlke, R. Li, & M. Orleans (Eds.), *Psychosocial Studies of the Individual's Changing Perspectives in Alzheimer's Disease* (pp. 104–130). Hershey, PA: IGI Global. doi:10.4018/978-1-4666-8478-2.ch005

Gardner, M. K., & Strayer, D. L. (2017). What Cognitive Psychology Can Tell Us About Educational Computer Games. In R. Zheng & M. Gardner (Eds.), *Handbook of Research on Serious Games for Educational Applications* (pp. 1–18). Hershey, PA: IGI Global. doi:10.4018/978-1-5225-0513-6.ch001

Garg, B., Khanna, P., & Khanna, A. (2017). Chronic Mental Illness and the Changing Scope of Intervention Strategies, Diagnosis, and Treatment in Child and Adolescent Population. In B. Prasad (Ed.), *Chronic Mental Illness and the Changing Scope of Intervention Strategies, Diagnosis, and Treatment* (pp. 258–269). Hershey, PA: IGI Global. doi:10.4018/978-1-5225-0519-8.ch014

Gautreau, C. S., Stang, K. K., Street, C., & Guillaume, A. (2014). Making the Move: Supporting Faculty in the Transition to Blended or Online Courses. *International Journal of Online Pedagogy and Course Design*, 4(1), 27–42. doi:10.4018/ijopcd.2014010103

Giannouli, V. (2017). Creativity and Giftedness: A Study of Attitudes. In N. Silton (Ed.), *Exploring the Benefits of Creativity in Education, Media, and the Arts* (pp. 179–197). Hershey, PA: IGI Global. doi:10.4018/978-1-5225-0504-4.ch009

Gikandi, J. W. (2015). Towards a Theory of Formative Assessment in Online Higher Education. In J. Keengwe (Ed.), *Handbook of Research on Educational Technology Integration and Active Learning* (pp. 292–316). Hershey, PA: IGI Global. doi:10.4018/978-1-4666-8363-1.ch014

Gikandi, J. W. (2017). Computer-Supported Collaborative Learning and Assessment: A Strategy for Developing Online Learning Communities in Continuing Education. In J. Keengwe & G. Onchwari (Eds.), *Handbook of Research on Learner-Centered Pedagogy in Teacher Education and Professional Development* (pp. 309–333). Hershey, PA: IGI Global. doi:10.4018/978-1-5225-0892-2.ch017

Gillow-Wiles, H., & Niess, M. L. (2015). Engaging Google Docs to Support Collaboration and Reflection in Online Teacher Education. In M. Niess & H. Gillow-Wiles (Eds.), *Handbook of Research on Teacher Education in the Digital Age* (pp. 635–662). Hershey, PA: IGI Global. doi:10.4018/978-1-4666-8403-4.ch024

Gillow-Wiles, H., & Niess, M. L. (2016). A Reconstructed Conception of Learner Engagement in Technology Rich Online Learning Environments. In M. Niess, S. Driskell, & K. Hollebrands (Eds.), *Handbook of Research on Transforming Mathematics Teacher Education in the Digital Age* (pp. 577–607). Hershey, PA: IGI Global. doi:10.4018/978-1-5225-0120-6.ch022

Golden, J. E., & Brown, V. (2017). A Holistic Professional Development Model: A Case Study to Support Faculty Transition to Online Teaching. In C. Martin & D. Polly (Eds.), *Handbook of Research on Teacher Education and Professional Development* (pp. 259–284). Hershey, PA: IGI Global. doi:10.4018/978-1-5225-1067-3.ch014

Goodson-Espy, T., & Poling, L. (2015). Interactive Whiteboards: Preparing Secondary Mathematics Teachers to Avoid Catch-22. In D. Polly (Ed.), *Cases on Technology Integration in Mathematics Education* (pp. 288–307). Hershey, PA: IGI Global. doi:10.4018/978-1-4666-6497-5.ch014

Gopalan, R. T. (2016). Intellectual Disability: From History to Recent Trends. In R. Gopalan (Ed.), *Handbook of Research on Diagnosing, Treating, and Managing Intellectual Disabilities* (pp. 1–10). Hershey, PA: IGI Global. doi:10.4018/978-1-5225-0089-6.ch001

Guan, S. (2014). Internet-Based Technology Use in Second Language Learning: A Systematic Review. *International Journal of Cyber Behavior, Psychology and Learning, 4*(4), 69–81. doi:10.4018/ijcbpl.2014100106

Gupta, S., Taneja, S., & Kumar, N. (2015). Redefining the Classroom: Integration of Open and Classroom Learning in Higher Education. In E. McKay & J. Lenarcic (Eds.), *Macro-Level Learning through Massive Open Online Courses (MOOCs)* (pp. 168–182). Hershey, PA: IGI Global. doi:10.4018/978-1-4666-8324-2.ch010

Hacker, D. J. (2017). The Role of Metacognition in Learning via Serious Games. In R. Zheng & M. Gardner (Eds.), *Handbook of Research on Serious Games for Educational Applications* (pp. 19–40). Hershey, PA: IGI Global. doi:10.4018/978-1-5225-0513-6.ch002

Hadjileontiadou, S. J., Dias, S. B., Diniz, J. A., & Hadjileontiadis, L. J. (2015). Understanding Online Learning Environments (OLEs). In Fuzzy Logic-Based Modeling in Collaborative and Blended Learning (pp. 18-50). Hershey, PA: IGI Global. doi:10.4018/978-1-4666-8705-9.ch002

Halder, S., & Mahato, A. (2017). Cognitive Remediation Therapy in Chronic Schizophrenia. In B. Prasad (Ed.), *Chronic Mental Illness and the Changing Scope of Intervention Strategies, Diagnosis, and Treatment* (pp. 292–307). Hershey, PA: IGI Global. doi:10.4018/978-1-5225-0519-8.ch016

Harkness, S. J. (2014). Program Administration and Implementation of an Online Learning Initiative at a Historically Black College University. In M. Orleans (Ed.), *Cases on Critical and Qualitative Perspectives in Online Higher Education* (pp. 44–60). Hershey, PA: IGI Global. doi:10.4018/978-1-4666-5051-0.ch003

Harrington, R. A., Driskell, S. O., Johnston, C. J., Browning, C. A., & Niess, M. L. (2016). Technological Pedagogical Content Knowledge: Preparation and Support of Mathematics Teachers. In M. Niess, S. Driskell, & K. Hollebrands (Eds.), *Handbook of Research on Transforming Mathematics Teacher Education in the Digital Age* (pp. 1–22). Hershey, PA: IGI Global. doi:10.4018/978-1-5225-0120-6.ch001

Heins, S., Heins, G., & Dick-Muehlke, C. (2015). Steve's Story: Living with Mild Cognitive Impairment. In C. Dick-Muehlke, R. Li, & M. Orleans (Eds.), *Psychosocial Studies of the Individual's Changing Perspectives in Alzheimer's Disease* (pp. 33–60). Hershey, PA: IGI Global. doi:10.4018/978-1-4666-8478-2.ch002

Ndinguri, E., Machtmes, K., Machtmes, R. J., & Hill, J. (2015). Exploring How Women Entrepreneurs Use Technology for Idea Generation. *International Journal of E-Entrepreneurship and Innovation*, *5*(2), 24–38. doi:10.4018/IJEEI.2015070102

Nguyen, C., Davis, H., Sharrock, G., & Hempsall, K. (2014). Realising the Potential of MOOCs in Developing Capacity for Tertiary Education Managers. *Information Resources Management Journal*, *27*(2), 47–60. doi:10.4018/irmj.2014040104

Nthomang, K. (2016). Inspiring Poor Women to Empower Themselves: Insights and Lessons from Botswana. *International Journal of Civic Engagement and Social Change*, *3*(2), 39–53. doi:10.4018/IJCESC.2016040103

Nwosu, M., Igwe, K., & Emezie, N. (2014). Women Artisans' Information Needs, Sources and Seeking Behaviour and the Implication for Empowerment in a Semi-Urban Area in Nigeria. *International Journal of Civic Engagement and Social Change*, *1*(4), 47–63. doi:10.4018/IJCESC.2014100103

Ojokoh, B. A., Adeola, O. S., Isinkaye, F. O., & Abraham, C. (2014). Career Choices in Information and Communication Technology among South Western Nigerian Women. *Journal of Global Information Management*, *22*(2), 48–77. doi:10.4018/jgim.2014040104

Ololube, N. P., Agbor, C. N., & Agabi, C. O. (2017). Effective Leadership and Management in Universities through Quality Management Models. In N. Baporikar (Ed.), *Innovation and Shifting Perspectives in Management Education* (pp. 224–245). Hershey, PA: IGI Global. doi:10.4018/978-1-5225-1019-2.ch010

Özbaş, M. (2016). Chaotic and Complex Situations in Girls' Education: Problems and Solutions. In Ş. Erçetin (Ed.), *Applied Chaos and Complexity Theory in Education* (pp. 1–10). Hershey, PA: IGI Global. doi:10.4018/978-1-5225-0460-3.ch001

Ozdemir, E. A., & Dikilitaş, K. (2016). Teachers' Professional Development in the Digitized World: A Sample Blended Learning Environment for Educational Technology Training. In K. Dikilitaş (Ed.), *Innovative Professional Development Methods and Strategies for STEM Education* (pp. 115–125). Hershey, PA: IGI Global. doi:10.4018/978-1-4666-9471-2.ch007

Palmeira, M. (2014). Frontline Employees' Self-Perception of Ageism, Sexism, and Lookism: Comparative Analyses of Prejudice and Discrimination in Fashion and Food Retailing. In F. Musso & E. Druica (Eds.), *Handbook of Research on Retailer-Consumer Relationship Development* (pp. 275–296). Hershey, PA: IGI Global. doi:10.4018/978-1-4666-6074-8.ch015

Parsa, F. (2016). Challenges of Iranian Women to Change the Gender Discriminatory Law. In N. Mahtab, S. Parker, F. Kabir, T. Haque, A. Sabur, & A. Sowad (Eds.), *Discourse Analysis as a Tool for Understanding Gender Identity, Representation, and Equality* (pp. 74–89). Hershey, PA: IGI Global. doi:10.4018/978-1-5225-0225-8.ch004

Patiño, B. E. (2017). New Generation Management by Convergence and Individual Identity: A Systemic and Human-Oriented Approach. In N. Baporikar (Ed.), *Innovation and Shifting Perspectives in Management Education* (pp. 119–143). Hershey, PA: IGI Global. doi:10.4018/978-1-5225-1019-2.ch006

Pereira, C. E. (2014). Emerging Digital Technologies and Women's Leadership in Global Business. In P. Smith & T. Cockburn (Eds.), *Impact of Emerging Digital Technologies on Leadership in Global Business* (pp. 255–279). Hershey, PA: IGI Global. doi:10.4018/978-1-4666-6134-9.ch014

Phiri, S. (2016). Political Dis-Empowerment of Women by ICTs: The Case of the Zambian Elections. In J. Wilson & N. Gapsiso (Eds.), *Overcoming Gender Inequalities through Technology Integration* (pp. 54–67). Hershey, PA: IGI Global. doi:10.4018/978-1-4666-9773-7.ch003

Pimpa, N., & Hooi, E. (2014). Modern Leadership in Singaporean and Thai Organizational Contexts. *International Journal of Knowledge-Based Organizations*, 4(4), 21–35. doi:10.4018/ijkbo.2014100102

Prescott, J., & Bogg, J. (2014). Issues Career Women Face. In *Gender Divide and the Computer Game Industry* (pp. 170–192). Hershey, PA: IGI Global. doi:10.4018/978-1-4666-4534-9.ch008

Rathore, A. K., Tuli, N., & Ilavarasan, P. V. (2016). Pro-Business or Common Citizen?: An Analysis of an Indian Woman CEO's Tweets. *International Journal of Virtual Communities and Social Networking*, 8(1), 19–29. doi:10.4018/IJVCSN.2016010102

Renna, P., Izzo, C., & Romaniello, T. (2016). The Business Process Management Systems to Support Continuous Improvements. In W. Nuninger & J. Châtelet (Eds.), *Handbook of Research on Quality Assurance and Value Management in Higher Education* (pp. 237–256). Hershey, PA: IGI Global. doi:10.4018/978-1-5225-0024-7.ch009

Ro, H. K., & McIntosh, K. (2016). Constructing Conducive Environment for Women of Color in Engineering Undergraduate Education. In U. Thomas & J. Drake (Eds.), *Critical Research on Sexism and Racism in STEM Fields* (pp. 23–48). Hershey, PA: IGI Global. doi:10.4018/978-1-5225-0174-9.ch002

Robby, M. A. (2014). Faculty and Chair Perceptions and Ratings about System-Wide Assessments in the Higher Colleges of Technology. In V. Wang (Ed.), *Advanced Research in Adult Learning and Professional Development: Tools, Trends, and Methodologies* (pp. 102–120). Hershey, PA: IGI Global. doi:10.4018/978-1-4666-4615-5.ch004

Roberts, C. (2017). Advancing Women Leaders in Academe: Creating a Culture of Inclusion. In S. Mukerji & P. Tripathi (Eds.), *Handbook of Research on Administration, Policy, and Leadership in Higher Education* (pp. 256–273). Hershey, PA: IGI Global. doi:10.4018/978-1-5225-0672-0.ch012

Runté, M., & Runté, R. (2017). The Evolving Discourse of the Purpose of Higher Education: The Rhetoric of Higher Education Reform. In S. Mukerji & P. Tripathi (Eds.), *Handbook of Research on Administration, Policy, and Leadership in Higher Education* (pp. 532–548). Hershey, PA: IGI Global. doi:10.4018/978-1-5225-0672-0.ch021

Samya, A. S. (2016). Diversity or Dilemma: The Cry for Social Freedom of MSM People Living in Dhaka City. In N. Mahtab, S. Parker, F. Kabir, T. Haque, A. Sabur, & A. Sowad (Eds.), *Revealing Gender Inequalities and Perceptions in South Asian Countries through Discourse Analysis* (pp. 1–19). Hershey, PA: IGI Global. doi:10.4018/978-1-5225-0279-1.ch001

Sanders, S. L., & Orbe, M. P. (2016). TIPs to Maximize Meaningful Professional Development Programs and Initiatives: A Case Study in Theoretically-Grounded Diversity Education. In C. Scott & J. Sims (Eds.), *Developing Workforce Diversity Programs, Curriculum, and Degrees in Higher Education* (pp. 235–257). Hershey, PA: IGI Global. doi:10.4018/978-1-5225-0209-8.ch013

Scott, C. L. (2016). The Diverse Voices Conference: Expanding Diversity Education Beyond the Classroom. In C. Scott, & J. Sims (Eds.), *Developing Workforce Diversity Programs, Curriculum, and Degrees in Higher Education* (pp. 62-73). Hershey, PA: IGI Global. doi:10.4018/978-1-5225-0209-8.ch004

Shambaugh, N. (2017). Ongoing and Systematic Academic Program Review. In S. Mukerji & P. Tripathi (Eds.), *Handbook of Research on Administration, Policy, and Leadership in Higher Education* (pp. 141–156). Hershey, PA: IGI Global. doi:10.4018/978-1-5225-0672-0.ch007

Shumilova, Y., & Cai, Y. (2016). Three Approaches to Competing for Global Talent: Role of Higher Education. In K. Bista & C. Foster (Eds.), *Global Perspectives and Local Challenges Surrounding International Student Mobility* (pp. 114–135). Hershey, PA: IGI Global. doi:10.4018/978-1-4666-9746-1.ch007

Sims, C. H. (2015). Genderized Workplace Lookism in the U.S. and Abroad: Implications for Organization and Career Development Professionals. In C. Hughes (Ed.), *Impact of Diversity on Organization and Career Development* (pp. 105–127). Hershey, PA: IGI Global. doi:10.4018/978-1-4666-7324-3.ch005

Smith, A. R. (2017). Ensuring Quality: The Faculty Role in Online Higher Education. In K. Shelton & K. Pedersen (Eds.), *Handbook of Research on Building, Growing, and Sustaining Quality E-Learning Programs* (pp. 210–231). Hershey, PA: IGI Global. doi:10.4018/978-1-5225-0877-9.ch011

Smith, C. R. (2015). Black, Female, and Foreign: The Triple-Invisibility of Afro-Caribbean Women in the Academy. In M. Zhou (Ed.), *Supporting Multiculturalism and Gender Diversity in University Settings* (pp. 74–100). Hershey, PA: IGI Global. doi:10.4018/978-1-4666-8321-1.ch005

Smyth, R., Bossu, C., & Stagg, A. (2016). Toward an Open Empowered Learning Model of Pedagogy in Higher Education. In S. Reushle, A. Antonio, & M. Keppell (Eds.), *Open Learning and Formal Credentialing in Higher Education: Curriculum Models and Institutional Policies* (pp. 205–222). Hershey, PA: IGI Global. doi:10.4018/978-1-4666-8856-8.ch011

Stevenson, C. N. (2016). Communicating across the Generations: Implications for Higher Education Leadership. In A. Normore, L. Long, & M. Javidi (Eds.), *Handbook of Research on Effective Communication, Leadership, and Conflict Resolution* (pp. 494–514). Hershey, PA: IGI Global. doi:10.4018/978-1-4666-9970-0.ch026

Swami, B. N., Gobona, T., & Tsimako, J. J. (2017). Academic Leadership: A Case Study of the University of Botswana. In N. Baporikar (Ed.), *Innovation and Shifting Perspectives in Management Education* (pp. 1–32). Hershey, PA: IGI Global. doi:10.4018/978-1-5225-1019-2.ch001

Timmerman, L. C., & Mulvihill, T. M. (2017). Department Chair Perspectives About Contingent Faculty in Higher Education: Leadership Theory. In S. Mukerji & P. Tripathi (Eds.), *Handbook of Research on Administration, Policy, and Leadership in Higher Education* (pp. 440–460). Hershey, PA: IGI Global. doi:10.4018/978-1-5225-0672-0.ch017

Tomos, F., Clark, A., Thurariaj, S., Balan, O. C., & Turner, D. (2016). The Emergence of Women Entrepreneurs and Communities of Practice within the Global Context. In S. Buckley, G. Majewski, & A. Giannakopoulos (Eds.), *Organizational Knowledge Facilitation through Communities of Practice in Emerging Markets* (pp. 85–113). Hershey, PA: IGI Global. doi:10.4018/978-1-5225-0013-1.ch005

Torok, R. (2016). The Role of Women from a Social Media Jihad Perspective: Wife or Warrior? In R. English & R. Johns (Eds.), *Gender Considerations in Online Consumption Behavior and Internet Use* (pp. 161–184). Hershey, PA: IGI Global. doi:10.4018/978-1-5225-0010-0.ch011

Toulassi, B. (2017). Educational Administration and Leadership in Francophone Africa: 5 Dynamics to Change Education. In S. Mukerji & P. Tripathi (Eds.), *Handbook of Research on Administration, Policy, and Leadership in Higher Education* (pp. 20–45). Hershey, PA: IGI Global. doi:10.4018/978-1-5225-0672-0.ch002

Tran, B. (2015). The Next Generation of Leaders: Women in Global Leaderships in Hotel Management Industry. In J. Feng, S. Stocklin, & W. Wang (Eds.), *Educational Strategies for the Next Generation Leaders in Hotel Management* (pp. 16–42). Hershey, PA: IGI Global. doi:10.4018/978-1-4666-8565-9.ch002

Tran, B. (2016). Culturally Gendered: The Institutionalization of Men and Masculinities in Society and Corporations. In N. Mahtab, S. Parker, F. Kabir, T. Haque, A. Sabur, & A. Sowad (Eds.), *Discourse Analysis as a Tool for Understanding Gender Identity, Representation, and Equality* (pp. 99–135). Hershey, PA: IGI Global. doi:10.4018/978-1-5225-0225-8.ch006

Tran, B. (2016). Gendered Social-Networking Organizations: A View of the Sexed Mentorship Relationships. *International Journal of Organizational and Collective Intelligence*, 6(2), 26–49. doi:10.4018/IJOCI.2016040103

Van Den Hoven, M., & Litz, D. R. (2016). Organizational Metaphors and the Evaluation of Higher Education Programs, Management Practices, and Change Processes: A UAE Case Study. In E. Espinosa (Ed.), *Systemic Knowledge-Based Assessment of Higher Education Programs* (pp. 43–68). Hershey, PA: IGI Global. doi:10.4018/978-1-5225-0457-3.ch004

Van Ryneveld, L. (2016). Introducing Educational Technology into the Higher Education Environment: A Professional Development Framework. In K. Dikilitaş (Ed.), *Innovative Professional Development Methods and Strategies for STEM Education* (pp. 126–136). Hershey, PA: IGI Global. doi:10.4018/978-1-4666-9471-2.ch008

Vargas-Hernández, J. G., & Ibarra, S. T. (2017). Evaluating Higher Education Institutions through Agency and Resource-Capabilities Theories: A Model for Measuring the Perceived Quality of Service. In N. Baporikar (Ed.), *Innovation and Shifting Perspectives in Management Education* (pp. 246–268). Hershey, PA: IGI Global. doi:10.4018/978-1-5225-1019-2.ch011

Whitehurst, J., & Vander Putten, J. (2014). Communication between Higher Education and Social Networking Sites. In C. Stevenson & J. Bauer (Eds.), *Building Online Communities in Higher Education Institutions: Creating Collaborative Experience* (pp. 1–22). Hershey, PA: IGI Global. doi:10.4018/978-1-4666-5178-4.ch001

Wittmer, J. L., & Rudolph, C. W. (2015). The Impact of Diversity on Career Transitions over the Life Course. In C. Hughes (Ed.), *Impact of Diversity on Organization and Career Development* (pp. 151–185). Hershey, PA: IGI Global. doi:10.4018/978-1-4666-7324-3.ch007

Wittmer, J. L., Werth, P. M., & Rudolph, C. W. (2016). Career Transitions and Trajectories for a Diverse Workforce: A Special Focus on Women and Older Workers. In J. Prescott (Ed.), *Handbook of Research on Race, Gender, and the Fight for Equality* (pp. 492–538). Hershey, PA: IGI Global. doi:10.4018/978-1-5225-0047-6.ch022

Wynne, C. W. (2016). Cultivating Leaders from Within: Transforming Workers into Leaders. In *Professional Development and Workplace Learning: Concepts, Methodologies, Tools, and Applications* (pp. 1675–1691). Hershey, PA: IGI Global. doi:10.4018/978-1-4666-8632-8.ch091

Xerri, D. (2014). Teachers' Use of Social Networking Sites for Continuing Professional Development. In G. Mallia (Ed.), *The Social Classroom: Integrating Social Network Use in Education* (pp. 441–464). Hershey, PA: IGI Global. doi:10.4018/978-1-4666-4904-0.ch022

Yuce, S. T., Agarwal, N., Wigand, R. T., Lim, M., & Robinson, R. S. (2014). Bridging Women Rights Networks: Analyzing Interconnected Online Collective Actions. *Journal of Global Information Management, 22*(4), 1–20. doi:10.4018/jgim.2014100101

Zgheib, P. W. (2015). Sexual Harassment Laws and Their Impact on the Work Environment. In *Business Ethics and Diversity in the Modern Workplace* (pp. 41–65). Hershey, PA: IGI Global. doi:10.4018/978-1-4666-7254-3.ch004

Zhou, C. (2017). Fostering Creative Problem Solvers in Higher Education: A Response to Complexity of Societies. In C. Zhou (Ed.), *Handbook of Research on Creative Problem-Solving Skill Development in Higher Education* (pp. 1–23). Hershey, PA: IGI Global. doi:10.4018/978-1-5225-0643-0.ch001

Zhou, C. (2017). Going Towards Adaption, Integration, and Co-Creation: A Conclusion to Developing Creative Problem Solving Skills in Higher Education. In C. Zhou (Ed.), *Handbook of Research on Creative Problem-Solving Skill Development in Higher Education* (pp. 533–540). Hershey, PA: IGI Global. doi:10.4018/978-1-5225-0643-0.ch024

Zhou, M. Y. (2015). Gender and Education: Equity and Equality in Post Mao China. In M. Zhou (Ed.), *Supporting Multiculturalism and Gender Diversity in University Settings* (pp. 56–73). Hershey, PA: IGI Global. doi:10.4018/978-1-4666-8321-1.ch004

About the Authors

Inna Piven is a Marketing Educator, Learning Designer, researcher, and business consultant. She received her Graduate Diploma in Education from The Far Eastern State University of Humanities (Russia) and Master of Business from Unitec Institute of Technology (New Zealand). Since 2011, Inna has been teaching a variety of marketing papers across polytechnics in New Zealand focusing on innovative approaches in course design and delivery. As a Learning Designer, she has been involved in undergraduate and post-graduate course development for different disciplines. Her research interests cover a range of business and educational topics related to social media. Inna has published journal articles and book chapters that include Journal of Retailing and Consumer Services, and Advances in E-Business Research (AEBR) Book Series by IGI Global. She has made numerous New Zealand and international conference presentations, and also served as a reviewer for marketing publications including Case Studies in Strategic Communication. In 2015 Inna won the "Excellence in Research and Enterprise" award for her research and student project supervision.

Robyn Gandell is an academic advisor at Unitec Institute of Technology and a doctoral candidate at the University of Auckland. In her tertiary education Robyn has been awarded a BSc with the Senior Prize in Pure Mathematics, a Graduate Diploma in Secondary Teaching, and a Post-Graduate Diploma, with Distinction, in Mathematics Education and a Diploma in Physiotherapy. Robyn has taught dance, mathematics, and physics, in both secondary and tertiary education, is a Senior Fellow of the Higher Education Academy in the UK and has teaching awards for Lecturer of the Year and Learning and Teaching Innovation from Unitec Institute of Technology. Robyn's current doctoral research explores mathematical problem solving and embodied mathematical thinking.

Maryann Lee has worked within tertiary educational environments in the area of e-learning and learning design over the last 15 years. One of her key roles has been in course design and development, where she works with lecturers to create course that are supported by the use of digital learning tools for blended and online learning. Her particular research interest lies in engaging Māori and Indigenous students in digital spaces and online learning communities. Maryann completed her Masters of Professional Studies in Education at the University of Auckland, New Zealand in 2015. Maryann has a Māori-Chinese heritage and currently resides in Auckland New Zealand.

Ann Simpson is currently an academic advisor at Unitec Institute of Technology, New Zealand and has a doctorate of education candidate at Massey University, New Zealand. Ann has worked extensively in learning and development in the IT industry in Silicon Valley as well as in New Zealand. She also holds an M.A. in Instructional Technologies from San Francisco State University. Ann's area of research for her doctorate focuses on the study of dialogic learning in blended tertiary classrooms.

Index

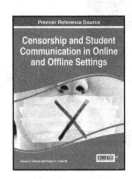

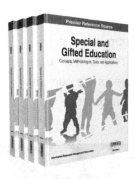
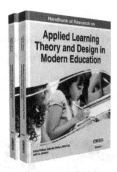

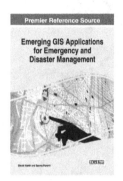

Printed in the United States
By Bookmasters